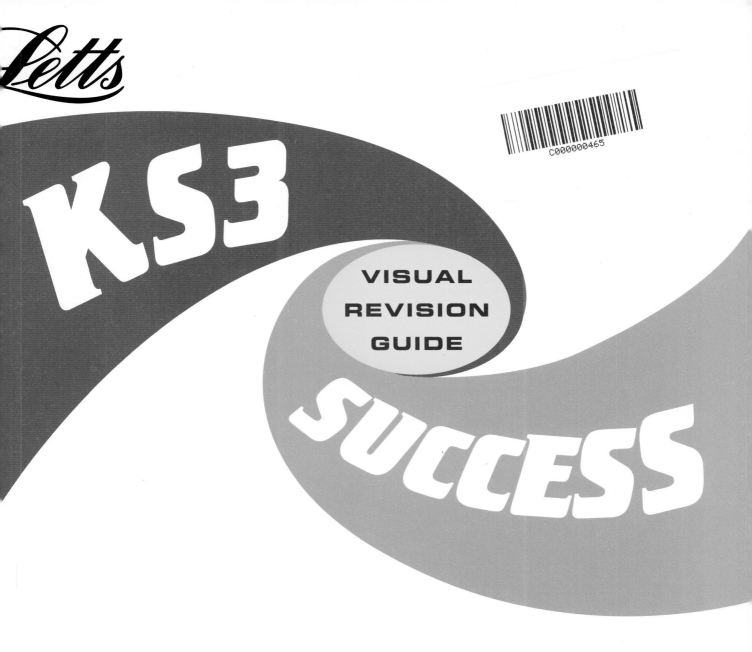

Letts

KS3

VISUAL REVISION GUIDE

SUCCESS

MATHEMATICS

Author

Fiona Mapp

CONTENTS

NUMBER

ALGEBRA

SHAPE, SPACE AND MEASURES

Revised

HANDLING DATA

Revised

PLACE VALUE IN WHOLE NUMBERS

Each digit in a number has a <u>place value</u>.
The size of the number depends on its place value.
The place value changes by a factor of 10 as you <u>move</u> from one column to the next.

These gaps make big numbers easier to read.

40
The place value is <u>ten</u> for this digit 4.

ten millions	millions	hundred thousands	ten thousands	thousands	hundreds	tens	units	
						6	2	sixty two
					5	3	8	five hundred and thirty eight
				4	2	9	2	four thousand, two hundred and ninety two
			5	3	4	0	0	fifty three thousand and four hundred
		2	3	6	5	2	0	two hundred and thirty six thousand, five hundred and twenty
4	3	9	5	0	2	5		four million, three hundred and ninety five thousand and twenty five

Always read the numbers from left to right.

NUMBERS 1

ORDERING WHOLE NUMBERS

• *When putting numbers into order of size, it is a good idea to put the numbers into groups with the same number of digits.*
• *For each group, arrange the numbers in order of size depending on the place value of the digits.*

EXAMPLE

Arrange these numbers in order of size, smallest first.
26, 502, 794, 3627, 4209, 4390, 7, 86, 28, 114

This becomes
7, 26, 28, 86, 114, 502, 794, 3627, 4209, 4390

Examiner's Top Tip
Knowing your multiplication tables is the key to success! Practise your tables and ask a friend to test you.

MULTIPLES AND ODD AND EVEN NUMBERS

ODD AND EVEN NUMBERS

All whole numbers are either <u>odd</u> or <u>even</u>.

1 <u>2</u> 3 <u>4</u> 5 <u>6</u> 7 <u>8</u> 9 <u>10</u> 11 <u>12</u> 13 <u>14</u> 15 <u>16</u> 17 <u>18</u> 19 <u>20</u> 21 <u>22</u> 23 <u>24</u>

The numbers in <u>red</u> are even. The numbers in <u>blue</u> are odd.

MULTIPLES

These are just the numbers in <u>multiplication</u> <u>tables</u>.

For example, multiples of 6 are 6, 12, 18, 24, . . .

The table below is the multiplication or <u>times</u> <u>tables</u> up to 10. You are expected to know these tables.

X	1	2	3	4	5	6	7	8	9	10
1	1	2	3	4	5	6	7	8	9	10
2	2	4	6	8	10	12	14	16	18	20
3	3	6	9	12	15	18	21	24	27	30
4	4	8	12	16	20	24	28	32	36	40
5	5	10	15	20	25	30	35	40	45	50
6	6	12	18	24	30	36	42	48	54	60
7	7	14	21	28	35	42	49	56	63	70
8	8	16	24	32	40	48	56	64	72	80
9	9	18	27	36	45	54	63	72	81	90
10	10	20	30	40	50	60	70	80	90	100

The multiplication table can also help you with <u>division</u>.

Try and get someone to test you on your tables to help you learn them.

EXAMPLE

$4 \times 6 = 24$ so $24 \div 6 = 4$

and $24 \div 4 = 6$

QUICK TEST

1. Write down the even numbers between 10 and 20.

2. Write down the multiples of 6 between 20 and 40.

3. Write this number 27 402 in words.

1. 10, 12, 14, 16, 18, 20   2. 24, 30, 36   3. Twenty seven thousand four hundred and two

NUMBERS ②

FACTORS

These are whole numbers which divide exactly into other numbers. For example, factors of 12 are

1, 2, 3, 4, 6, 12.

PRIME NUMBERS

These are numbers which only have two factors, 1 and itself. Prime numbers up to 20 are

2, 3, 5, 7, 11, 13, 17, 19.

NOTE that 1 is not a prime number.

RECIPROCALS

The reciprocal of a number $\frac{a}{x}$ is $\frac{x}{a}$

EXAMPLE

The reciprocal of $\frac{2}{3}$ is $\frac{3}{2}$

The reciprocal of 4 is $\frac{1}{4}$, since $4 = \frac{4}{1}$

Make sure you know the prime numbers up to 20.

PRIME FACTORS

These are <u>factors</u> which are <u>prime</u>. Some numbers can be written as a <u>product</u> of their prime factors.

EXAMPLE

The diagram shows the prime factors of 50.
- Divide 50 by its first prime factor 2.
- Divide 25 by its first prime factor 5.
- Keep on going until the final number is prime.

As a product of its prime factors.
50 may be written as:

$2 \times 5 \times 5 = 50$

or $\quad 2 \times 5^2 = 50$

in <u>index</u> notation (using powers).

Examiner's Top Tip
LEVEL 7
When writing the prime factors of a number, remember to write the final answer as a multiplication.

HIGHEST COMMON FACTOR (HCF)

The <u>largest factor</u> that two numbers have in common is called the <u>HCF</u>.

EXAMPLE

Find the HCF of 84 and 360.
Write the numbers as products of their prime factors.

$84 = 2 \times 2 \times 3 \times 7$
$360 = 2 \times 2 \times 2 \times 3 \times 3 \times 5$

Ring the factors in common.
These give the HCF = $2 \times 2 \times 3 = 12$

LOWEST COMMON MULTIPLE (LCM)

This is the <u>lowest</u> number which is a <u>multiple</u> of two numbers.

EXAMPLE

Find the LCM of 6 and 8
$8 = 2 \times 2 \times 2$
$6 = \qquad 2 \times 3$
8 and 6 have a common prime factor of 2, this is only counted once.
LCM of 6 and 8 is $2 \times 2 \times 2 \times 3 = 24$

INDEX NOTATION

- An <u>index</u> is sometimes known as a <u>power</u>.
6^4 is read as <u>6 to the power 4</u>. It means $6 \times 6 \times 6 \times 6$.
5^6 is read as <u>5 to the power 6</u>. It means $5 \times 5 \times 5 \times 5 \times 5 \times 5$.

known as the base ———— a^b —— known as the index or power

- The base is the value which has to be multiplied. The index indicates how many times.

POWERS ON A CALCULATOR DISPLAY

The value 5×10^6 means
$$5 \times 10 \times 10 \times 10 \times 10 \times 10 \times 10$$
$$= 5\ 000\ 000.$$
On a calculator display 5×10^6 would look like $5^{\ 06}$.
On a calculator display 7×10^{19} would look like $7^{\ 19}$.

SQUARES AND CUBES

Square and cube numbers can be represented by a diagram.

- **Anything to the <u>power 2</u> is <u>square</u>. For example, $3^2 = 3 \times 3 = 9$**
- **Anything to the <u>power 3</u> is <u>cube</u>. For example, $4^3 = 4 \times 4 \times 4 = 64$**

Square numbers include:

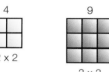

1	4	9	16
1 x 1	2 x 2	3 x 3	4 x 4

Cube numbers include:

1	8	27
1 x 1 x 1	2 x 2 x 2	3 x 3 x 3

SQUARE ROOTS AND CUBE ROOTS

$\sqrt{}$ is the <u>square root sign</u>. Taking the square root is the <u>opposite of squaring</u>, for example, $\sqrt{36} = 6$ since $6 \times 6 = 36$.
$\sqrt[3]{}$ is the <u>cube root sign</u>. Taking the cube root is the <u>opposite of cubing</u>, for example, $\sqrt[3]{64} = 4$ since $4 \times 4 \times 4 = 64$.

QUICK TEST

1.
1 2 3 4
5 6 7 8
9 10 11 12

From the above numbers write down:

a) Any multiples of 3   b) Any prime numbers.   c) Factors of 20.

d) Even numbers.   e) Numbers divisible by 5.

2. Work out without a calculator:

a) $\sqrt{100}$ b) 8^2 c) $\sqrt{64}$ d) 2^3

3. Find the HCF and LCM of 20 and 25.

LEVEL 7

1. a) 3, 6, 9, 12   b) 2, 3, 5, 7, 11   c) 1, 2, 4, 5, 10   d) 2, 4, 6, 8, 10, 12   e) 5, 10   2. a) 10   b) 64   c) 8   d) 8   3. HCF = 5   LCM = 100

DIRECTED NUMBERS

- These are numbers which may be positive or negative. Positive are above zero, negative are below zero.

Negative numbers ←——— ———→ **Positive numbers**

$$-8 \quad -7 \quad -6 \quad -5 \quad -4 \quad -3 \quad -2 \quad -1 \quad 0 \quad 1 \quad 2 \quad 3 \quad 4 \quad 5 \quad 6 \quad 7 \quad 8$$

- Negative numbers are commonly used to describe temperatures, i.e. –5°C means 5°C below zero.

EXAMPLES
–4 is smaller than 4
–2 is bigger than –5

EXAMPLE
Arrange these temperatures in order of size, smallest first.
–6°C, 4°C, –10°C, 3°C, 2°C, –1°C
Arranged in order: –10°C, –6°C, –1°C, 2°C, 3°C, 4°C

Examiner's Top Tip
- If you find working with directed numbers difficult, sketch a quick number line to help you.
- The rules of multiplication/division need to be remembered; you could quite easily use these laws when multiplying out brackets in algebra.

POSITIVE AND NEGATIVE + NUMBERS –

NEGATIVE NUMBERS ON THE CALCULATOR

The $+/-$ or $(-)$ key on the calculator gives a negative number.
For example, to get –2, press 2 $+/-$ or $(-)$ 2
This represents the sign.

EXAMPLE
–6 – (–3) = –3
can be keyed in the calculator like this; depending on your make of calculator

Make sure you know how to enter it in your calculator.

6 $+/-$ $-$ 3 $+/-$ $=$
sign — operation — sign

MULTIPLYING AND DIVIDING DIRECTED NUMBERS

(+) × (+) = +
(–) × (–) = +
(+) × (–) = –
(–) × (+) = –
(+) ÷ (+) = +
(–) ÷ (–) = +
(+) ÷ (–) = +
(–) ÷ (+) = –

- *Multiply and divide the numbers as normal.*
- *Find the sign for the answer using these rules:*

two **like** signs (both + or both –) give **positive**
two **unlike** signs (one + and the other –) give **negative**.

Multiply or divide as normal, then put in the sign.

EXAMPLES
–6 x (+4) = –24   –3 x (–4) = 12   –24 ÷ (–2) = 12   15 ÷ (–3) = –5

ADDING AND SUBTRACTING DIRECTED NUMBERS

- When adding and subtracting directed numbers it is helpful to draw a number line.

EXAMPLE
The temperature at 3 p.m. was 2°C; by 11 p.m. it had dropped by 7°C. What is the temperature at 11 p.m.?

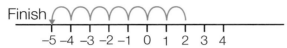

Finish
$$-5\ -4\ -3\ -2\ -1\ \ 0\ \ 1\ \ 2\ \ 3\ \ 4$$

The new temperature is –5°C.

EXAMPLE
Find the value of –2 – 7 (note the different uses of the minus sign).

$$-2 - 7$$

This represents the sign of the number, i.e. start at –2

This represents the operation of subtraction, i.e. move 7 places to the left

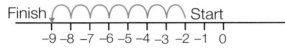

Finish   Start
$$-9\ -8\ -7\ -6\ -5\ -4\ -3\ -2\ -1\ \ 0$$

- When the number to be added (or subtracted) is negative, the normal direction of movement is reversed.

EXAMPLE
$$-6 - (-1)\text{ is the same as }-6 + 1 = -5.$$

The negative changes the direction.   Move 1 place to the right.

- When two (+) signs or two (–) signs are together then these rules are used:

$$+(+) = +$$ Like signs give $$+(-) = -$$ Unlike signs give
$$-(-) = +$$ } a positive. $$-(+) = -$$ } a negative.

EXAMPLES
$$-2 + (-3) = -2 - 3 = -5$$ $$-4 - (+4) = -4 - 4 = -8$$
$$5 - (-2) = 5 + 2 = 7$$ $$6 + (-2) = 6 - 2 = 4$$

QUICK TEST

1. The temperature inside the house is 12°C warmer than outside.

If the temperature outside is –5°C, what is the temperature inside?

2. Work out what the missing letters stand for:

a) 12 – A = –3   b) –6 + 10 = B   c) –9 x C = –36

d) –8 – (D) = 2   e) 120 ÷ (E) = –12   f) 14 + (F) = –6

1. 7°C 2. a) A = 15 b) B = 4 c) C = 4 d) D = –10 e) E = –10 f) F = –20

WORKING WITH NUMBERS

ADDITION AND SUBTRACTION

When adding and subtracting numbers, remember that their place values must line up, one on top of the other.

EXAMPLE
4279 + 368

| Line up the numbers first. |

```
 4279
  368 +
 4647
   1 1
```

Add the units, then 100s etc.

The one is carried here into the 10s column.

EXAMPLE
2791 – 365

```
  8 1
 2791
  365 –
 2426
```

Subtract the unit column. 1 – 5 won't work. We now borrow 10 from the next column. So the 9 becomes an 8 and the 1 becomes 11.

MULTIPLICATION AND DIVISION

Questions on multiplication and division will be difficult unless you know your times tables.

EXAMPLE

```
  274
    4 x
 1096
   2 1
```

Multiply the single digit number by each digit of the large number

When the answer is 10 or more carry the left digit to the next column.

Start with the units, then tens etc.

EXAMPLE

```
    403
 3 )1²209
```

Divide into the large number one digit at a time.

Put the result of each division on the top.

Carry the remainder if the small number will not go in exactly.

LONG DIVISION

A vase costs 74p. Tracey has £9.82 to spend. What is the maximum number of vases Tracey can buy? How much change does she have left? Do this calculation without using a calculator.

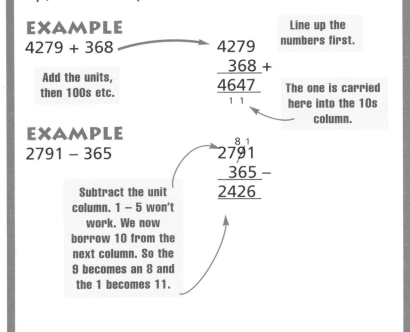

```
      13
 74 ) 98 2
      74 -
      242
      222 -
       20
```

Step 1: 74 goes into 98 once, put down 1

Step 2: Place 74 below 98

Step 3: Subtract 74 from 98

Step 4: Bring down the 2

Step 5: Divide 74 into 242, put down the 3

Step 6: 74 x 3 = 222

Step 7: 242 – 222 = remainder 20

Remember to change the units first.

Tracey can buy 13 vases and has 20p left over.

LONG MULTIPLICATION

EXAMPLE
A single plant costs 42p. Without a calculator work out the cost of 164 plants.

```
   164
    42 x
   328
     1
  6560 +
    2 1
  6888
```

Step 1: 164 x 2

Step 2: 164 x 40

Step 3: 328 + 6560

Cost = 6888p or £68.88.

Make your working out clear.

MULTIPLICATION AND DIVISION BY 10, 100, 1000

To <u>multiply</u> by 10, 100, 1 000 etc., move the decimal point one, two, three etc., columns to the left and put in zeros if necessary.

EXAMPLES

Ten thousands	Thousands	Hundreds	Tens	Units	.	Tens
			1	5	.	2
		1	5	2		
			5	3		
		5	3	0		
	1	1	5	.	2	
	1	5	2	0		
			5	3		
5	3	0	0	0		

x 10 = 152   **Each digit moves one place to the left.**

x 10 = 530   **Each digit moves one place to the left and put 0 in the units column.**

x 100 = 1520   **Each digit moves two places to the left and put 0 in the units column.**

x 1000 = 53000 **Each digit moves three places to the left and put 0 in the hundreds, tens and units column.**

To <u>divide</u> by 10, 100, 1 000 etc., move the decimal point one, two, three etc., places to the right.

EXAMPLES

$15.8 \div 10 = 1.58$ $18.2 \div 1 000 = 0.0182$

When multiplying by multiples of 10 (20, 30, 700 etc.) the same rules apply, except you multiply the numbers first then multiply by the power of 10.

EXAMPLES

$50 \times 30 = 1 500$

$24 \times 20 = 480$

When dividing by multiples of 10, the same rules apply, except you divide the numbers and then move the digits to the right.

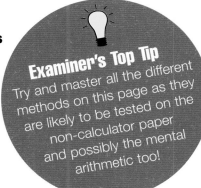

Examiner's Top Tip
Try and master all the different methods on this page as they are likely to be tested on the non-calculator paper and possibly the mental arithmetic too!

- -

QUICK TEST

Answer the following questions.

1. a) 279
      426 +

   b) 639
      148 –

   c) 276
        8 x

   d) 5)‾1 275

2. 279
    47 x

3. 37)‾925

4. Without a calculator work out:

a) 15.2 x 10   b) 6.3 x 100   c) 21 x 1 000   d) 25.2 ÷ 100

5. A tin of soup costs 68p. Work out the cost of 18 tins without using a calculator.

6. The cost of a trip is £10.25. If Mr Appleyard collects in £133.25 how many people are going on the trip? Work out without using a calculator.

1. a) 705 b) 491 c) 2208 d) 255   2. 13113   3. 25   4. a) 152 b) 630 c) 21000 d) 0.252   5. £12.24   6. 13

FRACTIONS

WHAT IS A FRACTION?

- A fraction is part of a whole one.
  $\frac{2}{5}$ means 2 parts out of 5.
- The top number is the <u>numerator</u>, the bottom one is the <u>denominator</u>.
- A fraction like $\frac{2}{5}$ is called a <u>proper</u> <u>fraction</u>.
- A fraction like $\frac{12}{7}$ is called an <u>improper</u> <u>fraction</u>.
- A fraction like $1\frac{4}{9}$ is called a <u>mixed</u> <u>number</u>.

If the numerator and the denominator are the same, then it is a whole one, i.e. $\frac{5}{5} = 1$.

ADDITION AND SUBTRACTION OF FRACTIONS

The example shows the basic principles of adding and subtracting fractions.

EXAMPLE

$\frac{1}{8} + \frac{3}{4}$ First make the denominators the same.

$\frac{1}{8} + \frac{6}{8}$ Replace $\frac{3}{4}$ with $\frac{6}{8}$ so that the denominators are now the same.

$= \frac{7}{8}$ Add the numerators $1 + 6 = 7$

<u>Do not add</u> the denominators.

The denominator stays the same number.

$$\overset{\times 2}{\frac{3}{4}} = \frac{6}{8}$$
$$\times 2$$

EXAMPLE

$\frac{3}{4} - \frac{3}{16}$ First make the denominators the same.

$\frac{3}{4}$ is equivalent to $\frac{12}{16}$

$\frac{12}{16} - \frac{3}{16}$ Replace $\frac{3}{4}$ with $\frac{12}{16}$

Subtract the numerators but not the denominators.

$= \frac{9}{16}$ The denominator stays the same number.

$$\overset{\times 4}{\frac{3}{4}} = \frac{12}{16}$$
$$\times 4$$

PROPORTIONAL CHANGES WITH FRACTIONS

FRACTIONS OF A QUANTITY

The word <u>of</u> means <u>multiply</u>.

EXAMPLE

In a class of 40 students, $\frac{2}{5}$ of them are left-handed. How many are left-handed?

$\frac{2}{5}$ of 40 means $\frac{2}{5} \times 40 = 16$ students

On the calculator key in:

$$2 \div 5 \times 40 =$$

Alternatively divide 40 by 5 to find $\frac{1}{5}$ then multiply by 2 to find $\frac{2}{5}$

EXAMPLE

The table shows some information about pupils in a school.

	Non-vegetarian	Vegetarian
Girls	147	62
Boys	183	41

There are 433 pupils in the school $(147 + 62 + 183 + 41)$.

a) What fraction are vegetarian?

b) What fraction of the boys are not vegetarian?

a) Vegetarian = $62 + 41 = 103$

    Fraction = $\frac{103}{433}$

b) Boys = $(183 + 41) = 224$

    Fraction = $\frac{183}{224}$

EQUIVALENT FRACTIONS

$\frac{1}{2}$

$\frac{2}{4}$

- These are fractions which have the same value.

EXAMPLE
From the diagram it can be seen that $\frac{1}{2} = \frac{2}{4}$

- Fractions can be changed into their equivalent by either <u>multiplying</u> or <u>dividing</u> the numerator and denominator by the same amount.

EXAMPLES
$\frac{7}{9} = \frac{?}{27}$

$\frac{35}{50} = \frac{7}{?}$

$\frac{7}{9} = \frac{21}{27}$

Multiply the top and bottom by 3.

$\frac{35}{50} = \frac{7}{10}$

Divide the top and bottom by 5.

SIMPLIFYING FRACTIONS
Fractions can be <u>simplified</u> if the numerator and the denominator have a common factor.

EXAMPLE
Simplify $\frac{12}{18}$.
6 is the highest factor of both 12 and 18.
Divide both the top and bottom number by 6.

$\frac{12}{18} = \frac{2}{3}$

So $\frac{12}{18}$ is simplified to $\frac{2}{3}$.

Using the fraction key on the calculator

$a^{b/c}$ is the fraction key on the calculator.

EXAMPLE
$\frac{20}{30}$ is keyed in as $\boxed{2\,0}\;\boxed{a^{b/c}}\;\boxed{3\,0}$
This is displayed as $\boxed{20 \lrcorner 30}$ or $\boxed{20 \ulcorner 30}$.
The calculator will automatically cancel down fractions when the $\boxed{=}$ key is pressed. For example, $\frac{20}{30}$ becomes $\boxed{2 \lrcorner 3}$ or $\boxed{2 \ulcorner 3}$.
<u>This means two-thirds</u>
A display of $\boxed{1 \lrcorner 5 \lrcorner 7}$ means $1\frac{5}{7}$.
If you now press $\boxed{shift}\;\boxed{a^{b/c}}$, it converts back to an improper fraction.
Check: you calculator may have a $\boxed{2nd}\;\boxed{Inv}$ instead of $\boxed{shift}$.

MULTIPLICATION AND DIVISION OF FRACTIONS

When multiplying and dividing fractions, write out whole or mixed numbers as improper fractions before starting. For example rewrite $2\frac{1}{2}$ as $\frac{5}{2}$.

EXAMPLE
$\frac{4}{7} \times \frac{2}{11} = \frac{8}{77}$

Multiply the numerators together.
Multiply the denominators together.

For division, change it into a multiplication by turning the second fraction upside down, (taking the reciprocal) and multiply both fractions together.

EXAMPLE
$\frac{7}{9} \div \frac{12}{18}$

Turn the $\frac{12}{18}$ upside down and multiply with $\frac{7}{9}$

$\frac{7}{9} \times \frac{18}{12} = \frac{126}{108} = 1\frac{1}{6}$

Rewrite back as a mixed number

QUICK TEST

1. Work out the missing values:

a) $\frac{7}{12} = \frac{14}{x}$ b) $\frac{125}{500} = \frac{y}{100}$ c) $\frac{19}{38} = \frac{76}{z}$

2. Work out the following:

a) $\frac{2}{9} + \frac{3}{27}$ b) $\frac{3}{5} - \frac{1}{4}$ c) $\frac{6}{9} \times \frac{72}{104}$ d) $\frac{8}{9} \div \frac{2}{3}$

3. $\frac{5}{8}$ of a class of 24 walk to school. How many pupils walk to school?

Examiner's Top Tip
Questions involving fractions are quite common on the non-calculator paper. Learn the quick way of finding a fraction of a quantity.

1. a) x = 24   b) y = 25   c) z = 152   2. a) $\frac{1}{3}$ b) $\frac{7}{20}$ c) $\frac{6}{13}$ d) $1\frac{1}{3}$ 3. 15 pupils

WHAT ARE DECIMALS?

- **A decimal point is used to separate whole number columns from fractional columns.**

EXAMPLE

Thousands	Hundreds	Tens	Units	Tenths	Hundredths	Thousandths
6	7	1	4 • 2	3		8

Decimal point

- The 2 means 2/10.
- The 3 means 3/100.
- The 8 means 8/1000.

RECURRING DECIMALS

- **A decimal that <u>recurs</u> is shown by placing a dot over the numbers that repeat.**

EXAMPLE

$0.66666\ldots = 0.\dot{6}$

$0.147147\ldots = 0.\dot{1}4\dot{7}$

Remember, hundredths are smaller than tenths, i.e. $\frac{3}{100}$ is smaller than $\frac{2}{10}$.

ORDERING DECIMALS

Have a quick check that all values are included.

When ordering decimals:
- First write them with the same number of figures after the decimal point.
- Then compare whole numbers, digits in the tenths place, digits in the hundredths place, and so on.

EXAMPLE

Arrange these numbers in order of size, smallest first:

4.27, 4.041, 4.7, 6.4, 2.19, 4.72

First rewrite them:

4.270, 4.041, 4.700, 6.400, 2.190, 4.720

The zero is smaller than the 2.

Then reorder them:

2.190   4.041   4.270   4.700   4.720   6.400

MULTIPLYING AND DIVIDING BY NUMBERS BETWEEN 0 AND 1

Examiner's Top Tip
Questions involving multiplication and division between 0 and 1 are common on the non-calculator pa... and the taped mental arithmetic t... In order to practise, it is wise t... write out a miniature test and check your answers with a calculator.

- When <u>multiplying</u> by numbers between 0 and 1, the result is <u>smaller</u> than the starting value.
- When <u>dividing</u> by numbers between 0 and 1, the result is <u>bigger</u> than the starting value.

EXAMPLES

$4 \times 0.1 = 0.4$

$4 \times 0.01 = 0.04$

$4 \times 0.001 = 0.004$

The result is <u>smaller</u> than the starting value.

$4 \div 0.1 = 40$

$4 \div 0.01 = 400$

$4 \div 0.001 = 4000$

The result is <u>bigger</u> than the starting value.

LEVEL 7

CALCULATIONS WITH DECIMALS

Calculations with decimals are similar to calculating with whole numbers.

EXAMPLES

1. Add together 6.21 and 4.9.

$$\begin{array}{r} 6.21 \\ + 4.90 \\ \hline 11.11 \\ {\scriptstyle 1} \end{array}$$

Put the decimal points under each other.

This is the same as 4.9.

The decimal points in the answer will be in line.

2. Subtract 6.2 from 12.81.

$$\begin{array}{r} 12.81 \\ 6.20 - \\ \hline 6.61 \end{array}$$

When adding or subtracting decimals make sure they have the same number of place values, i.e. 4.9 = 4.90.

3. Multiply 12.3 by 7.

$$\begin{array}{r} 12.3 \\ 7 \times \\ \hline 8\,6\,1 \\ {\scriptstyle 1\ 2} \end{array}$$

Multiply 123 by 7 = 861, ignore the decimal point
Since 12.3 has one number after the decimal point then so must the answer.

Answer = 86.1

4. Divide 25.8 by 6.

$$6\,\overline{\smash{\big)}\,25.8}\qquad \begin{array}{c}4.3\end{array}$$

When dividing, divide as normal, placing the decimal points in line.

Put the decimal points in line.

DECIMALS

QUICK TEST

Work out the answers to the following questions.

1. a) $\begin{array}{r} 27.9 \\ 143.07 + \end{array}$ b) $\begin{array}{r} 16.05 \\ 12.21 - \end{array}$ c) $\begin{array}{r} 27.8 \\ 3 \times \end{array}$ d) $4\,\overline{\smash{\big)}\,62.8}$

2. a) 60 x 30   d) 150 ÷ 5
    b) 6 x 30   e) 150 ÷ 0.5
    c) 0.6 x 30   f) 250 ÷ 0.005

LEVEL 7

3. Arrange these numbers in order of size, smallest first:

a) 0.62, 0.03, 0.84, 0.037

b) 27.06, 22.53, 22.507, 27.064

15

PERCENTAGES OF A QUANTITY

The word _of_ means _multiply_.

EXAMPLE
Find 15% of £650.
$\frac{15}{100} \times 650 = £97.50$

On the calculator key in
| 15 | ÷ | 100 | x | 650 | = |

Replace the word 'of' with a x sign. Rewrite the percentage as a fraction.

- If working out mentally, find 10% = 650 ÷ 10 = £65
  5% is half of £65 = £32.50
  Add the two together to give £97.50

EXAMPLE
Work out $17\frac{1}{2}$% of 360 without a calculator.
10%   of 360 = 36
5%   of 360 = 18
$2\frac{1}{2}$%   of 360 = 9
So $17\frac{1}{2}$% of 360 = 36 + 18 + 9 = 63

Examiner's Top Tip
Percentage questions appear frequently at KS3. If there is a percentage question on the non-calculator paper, work out what 10% is equal to as shown in the examples above.

PERCENTAGES ①

What is a percentage?
- **These are fractions with a denominator of 100.**
- **% is the percentage sign.**
- **75% means $\frac{75}{100}$ (this is equal to $\frac{3}{4}$).**

25%	
	75%

ONE QUANTITY AS A PERCENTAGE OF ANOTHER

RULE: To make the answer a PERCENTAGE, _multiply_ by 100%.

EXAMPLE
A survey shows that 26 people out of 45 preferred 'Supersuds' washing powder.
What percentage preferred Supersuds?

Make a fraction with the two numbers. Multiply by 100% to get a percentage.
$\frac{26}{45} \times 100\% = 57.\dot{7}\% = 57.8$ (1 d.p.)

On the calculator key in
| 26 | ÷ | 45 | x | 100 | = |

EXAMPLE
In a carton of milk, 6.2 g of the contents are fat.
If 2.5 g of the fat is saturated what percentage is this?

Make the fraction $\frac{2.5}{6.2} \times 100\% = 40.3\%$ (1 d.p.)   **x by 100%**

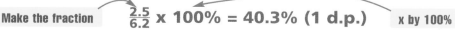

INCREASING AND DECREASING BY A PERCENTAGE

Percentages will often appear in real life problems.
You will often need to find the new value when the amount has been increased or decreased by a percentage.

EXAMPLE
A new car was bought for £8600. After 2 years, it had lost 30% of its value.
Work out the value of the car after 2 years using a non-calculator method.

$100\% = £8600$

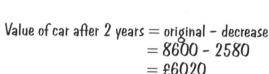

To find 10% remember to ÷ by 10!

$10\% = 8600 \div 10$
$\qquad = £860$

$30\% = 860 \times 3$
$\qquad = £2580$

Value of car after 2 years = original − decrease
$\qquad\qquad\qquad\qquad = 8600 - 2580$
$\qquad\qquad\qquad\qquad = £6020$

EXAMPLE
In 1998 the average price of a 3 bedroomed house was £72 000.
In 2001, the average price of a 3 bedroomed house had risen by 27%.
Work out the average price in 2001.

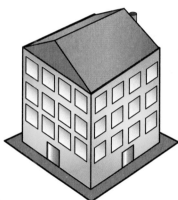

$100\% = £72\,000$
Increase $= 27\%$ of £72 000
$\qquad\qquad = \frac{27}{100} \times 72\,000 = £19\,440$

Remember 'of' means X.

Average price of house is now $= £72\,000 + £19\,440$
$\qquad\qquad\qquad\qquad\qquad = £91\,440$

Remember to answer the whole question!

QUICK TEST

1. Out of the 30 people at a bus stop, 10% wear glasses. How many people wear glasses?
2. 25% of the students in year 9 choose Maths as their favourite subject. If there are 140 students in the year, how many choose Maths?
3. If 20% of a number is 8 what is the number?
4. There are 62 cars in a car park: 14 are white. What percentage are white?
5. The top mark in a Maths test was 59 out of 72. Write this as a percentage.
6. A jumper costs £60. If it is reduced by 15% in a sale how much does it now cost?
7. The number of people who go swimming in the morning was 30. If this rose by 20%, how many now go swimming in the morning?

1. 3   2. 35   3. 40   4. 22.6%   5. 82%   6. £51   7. 36 people

REPEATED PERCENTAGE CHANGE

EXAMPLE

A clothing shop has a sale.
For each day of the sale, prices were reduced by 20% of the prices on the day before.
A jumper had a price of £45 on Monday.
If the sale starts on Tuesday, how much would Mary pay for the jumper if she bought it on Wednesday?

Monday price = £45

Make sure you do not do 2 x 20 = 40% reduction over 2 days.

Tuesday reduction = $\frac{20}{100}$ x 45 = £9

New price = £45 – £9 = £36

Wednesday reduction = $\frac{20}{100}$ x 36 = £7.20

New price = £36 – £7.20 = £28.80

Mary paid £28.80

Show your working clearly. Make sure these problems are worked out step by step.

LEVEL 7

EXAMPLE

A car is bought in 1998 for £10 500.
Each year the car depreciates (goes down) in value by 8%.
How much is the car worth after three years?

1998 £10 500

1999 $\frac{8}{100}$ x £10 500 = £840
New value = 10 500 – 840 = £9660

2000 $\frac{8}{100}$ x 9660 = £772.80
New value = 9660 – 772.80 = £8887.20

2001 $\frac{8}{100}$ x 8887.20 = £710.98
(nearest penny)

Car is worth £8887.20 – 710.98
= £8176.22

PROFIT AND LOSS

LEVEL 7

- **If you buy an article, the price you pay is the <u>cost</u> price.**
- **If you sell the article, the price you sell it for is the <u>selling</u> price.**
- **<u>Profit</u> (or <u>loss</u>) is the difference between the cost price and the selling price.**

You can write the profit or loss as a percentage of the original price.

Percentage profit = $\frac{profit}{original\ price}$ x 100%

Percentage loss = $\frac{loss}{original\ price}$ x 100%

EXAMPLE

A shop bought a television for £350. A customer later buys the television for £680. Find the percentage profit.

**Profit = £680 – £350
= £330**

Percentage profit = $\frac{profit}{original\ price}$ x 100%

$= \frac{330}{350}$ x 100%

= 94% profit

EXAMPLE

*Jacqueline bought a sofa for £569, but later sold it for £352.
Calculate her percentage loss.*

**Loss = £569 – £352
= £217**

Percentage loss = $\frac{217}{569}$ x 100%

= 38.1% loss

TAXATION

- Value Added Tax (VAT) is the amount added to bills for services and purchases.
- Currently VAT is $17\frac{1}{2}$%.

EXAMPLE

The price of a computer is £1150 plus VAT at $17\frac{1}{2}$%.
Work out the final cost inclusive of VAT.

VAT: 17.5% of £1150

$\frac{17.5}{100}$ x £1150 = £201.25

Those 'percentages of' questions again!

Total cost = £1150 + £201.25
       = £1351.25

This can be calculated by multiplying by $\frac{(100 + 17.5)}{100}$ i.e 1.175 - this is known as a <u>multiplier</u>.

INCOME TAX

A percentage of a taxable part of a wage is taken as Income Tax.

EXAMPLE

Rhysian earns £16000 a year. £12745 of her income is taxed at 23%.
How much income tax does she pay?

23% of £12745

$\frac{23}{100}$ x 12745 = £2931.35

Examiner's Top Tip
When answering questions that involve profit and loss, remember:
- multiply by 100%
- divide by the original or cost price. These are similar to percentage of questions.

PERCENTAGES ②

QUICK TEST

(c) 1. A house is bought for £65 000. Each year it rises in value by 10%.
How much is the house worth 3 years later?

(c) 2. Work out the percentage profit or loss on these items:

a) cost price £120, selling price £75

b) cost price £204, selling price £263

c) cost price £144, selling price £128.

(c) 3. VAT is added to a telephone bill of £72.40. Find the total amount to be paid.

1. £86 515   2. a) 37.5%   b) 28.9%   c) 11.1%   3. £85.07

COMMONLY KNOWN EQUIVALENCES

Fractions, decimals and percentages all mean the same thing but are just written in a different way.

The table shows:
- some common fractions and their equivalents which you need to learn.

- how to convert

fractions $\xrightarrow{\text{to}}$ decimals $\xrightarrow{\text{to}}$ percentages.

Fraction	Decimal	Percentage
$\frac{1}{2}$ $\xrightarrow{1 \div 2}$	0.5 $\xrightarrow{\text{x 100%}}$	50%
$\frac{1}{3}$	$0.\dot{3}$	$33.\dot{3}$%
$\frac{2}{3}$	$0.\dot{6}$	$66.\dot{6}$%
$\frac{1}{4}$	0.25	25%
$\frac{3}{4}$	0.75	75%
$\frac{1}{5}$	0.2	20%
$\frac{1}{8}$	0.125	12.5%
$\frac{3}{8}$	0.375	37.5%
$\frac{1}{10}$	0.1	10%
$\frac{1}{100}$	0.01	1%

EQUIVALENCES BETWEEN FRACTIONS, DECIMALS AND PERCENTAGES

ORDERING DIFFERENT NUMBERS

When putting fractions, decimals and percentages in order of size, it is best to change them all to <u>decimals</u> first.

Make sure you put the values in the order the question says.

EXAMPLE
Place in order of size, smallest first:
$\frac{1}{4}$, 0.241, 29%, 64%, $\frac{1}{3}$

$0.25, 0.241, 0.29, 0.6\dot{4}, 0.3\dot{3}$	Put into decimals first
$0.241, 0.25, 0.29, 0.3\dot{3}, 0.64$	Now order
$0.241, \frac{1}{4}, 29\%, \frac{1}{3}, 64\%$	Now rewrite in its original form

Examiner's Top Tip
Get a friend to test you on the equivalences between fractions, decimals and percentages because you need to learn them.

QUICK TEST

1. Complete the table.

Fraction (simplest form)	Decimal	Percentage
		75%
$\frac{2}{5}$		
	$0.\dot{3}$	
	0.6	
		20%

2. Arrange in order of size, smallest first:

$\frac{2}{3}$, 0.25, $\frac{5}{9}$, 84%, $\frac{9}{10}$

USING A CALCULATOR

ORDER OF OPERATIONS

<u>Bodmas</u> is a made up word which helps you to remember the order in which calculations take place.   B O D M A S

Brackets over Division Multiplication Addition Subtraction

This just means that brackets are carried out first, then the others are done in order.

EXAMPLES - $(2 + 4) \times 3 = 18$ $6 + 2 \times 4 = 14$ ← Not 32 because multiplication is done first.

INTERPRETING THE CALCULATOR DISPLAY

Don't forget to put the zero on the end, i.e. £6.7 is £6.70.

When questions involve money the following points need to be remembered:
- A display of 6.7 means £6.70 (six pounds seventy pence).
- A display of 5.03 means £5.03 (five pounds three pence).
- A display of 0.82 means £0.82 or 82 pence.
- A display of 6.2934 needs to be rounded to 2 d.p., i.e. £6.29.

CALCULATING POWERS

y^x or x^y is used for calculating powers such as 2^7.

- Use the power key on the calculator to work out 2^7.
- Write down the calculator keys used.
- Check you obtain the answer 128.

IMPORTANT CALCULATOR KEYS

This calculator is made up just to show you some of the important calculator keys. Make sure you know how your calculator works.

Make sure you understand how to use your calculator.

Shift or 2nd or Inv allow 2nd functions to be carried out.

− or +/− changes positive numbers to negative ones.

bracket keys

often puts the ×10 part in when working in standard form.

pressing shift EXP often gives π

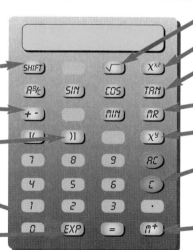

square root

square button

trigonometric buttons

memory keys

works out powers.

cancels only the last key you have pressed.

memory keys

EXAMPLE

$$\frac{15 \times 10 + 46}{9.3 \times 2.1} = 10.04 \ (2 \ d.p.)$$

This may be keyed in as:
[(... 15 × 10 + 46 ...)] ÷ [(... 9.3 × 2.1 ...)] =

The above could be as easily done using the memory keys. Try writing down the key sequence for yourself.

QUICK TEST

Work these out on your calculator.

1. a) $\dfrac{6.2 + (4.6)^2}{\sqrt{3.2} \times 1.7}$ b) $\dfrac{\sqrt{9.4} - 2.7}{6.1 + 8.2}$ c) $\dfrac{27.1 \times 6.4}{9.3 + 2.7}$ d) $\dfrac{(9.3)^4}{2.7 \times 3.6}$

2. Jonathan's calculator display shows 1.52^{06}. **Write down what the display means.**

1.a) 11.73 (2 d.p.) b) 0.026 (3 d.p.) c) 14.45 (2 d.p.) d) 769.6 (1 d.p.)

ROUNDING NUMBERS TO THE NEAREST TEN, HUNDRED, THOUSAND

Large numbers are often approximated to the nearest ten, hundred, thousand etc.

ROUNDING TO THE NEAREST TEN
Look at the digit in the <u>units</u> column. If it is less than 5, round down. If it is 5 or more, round up.

EXAMPLE
Round 568 to the nearest ten.

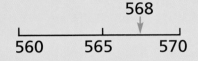

568 is closer to 570 than 560.

There is an 8 in the units column, so round up to 570.
568 is 570 to the nearest ten.

ROUNDING TO THE NEAREST HUNDRED
Look at the digit in the tens column. If it is less than 5, round down. If it is 5 or more, round up.

EXAMPLE
Round 2650 to the nearest hundred

There is a 5 in the tens column, so round up to 2700
2650 is 2700 to the nearest hundred.

ROUNDING TO THE NEAREST THOUSAND
**Look at the digits in the hundreds column.
The same rules apply as before.**

Sketch a number line if it helps.

EXAMPLE
Round 16420 to the nearest thousand. 16 000   16 500   17 000

16 420

There is a 4 in the hundreds column, so round down to 16 000.
16 420 is 16 000 to the nearest thousand.

DECIMAL PLACES (D.P.)

When rounding to a specified number of decimal places:
- look at the last digit that is wanted (if rounding 8.347 to 2 d.p. look at the 4 – second decimal place)
- look at the number next to it (look at the number not needed, i.e. the 7)
- if it is 5 or more round up the last digit (7 is greater than 5, so round the 4 up to a 5)
- if it is <u>less than 5</u>, the digit remains the <u>same</u>
- so to 2dp 8.347 = 8.35.

EXAMPLES
16.5<u>9</u> = 16.6 to 1 d.p.
8.43<u>5</u> = 8.44 to 2 d.p.
12.3<u>4</u> = 12.3 to 1 d.p.

SIGNIFICANT FIGURES (S.F. OR SIG. FIG.)

Apply the same rule as with decimal places. If the next digit is 5 or more, round up. The first significant figure is the first digit which is not a zero. The 2nd, 3rd, 4th, . . . significant figures follow on after the first digit. They may or may not be zeros.

EXAMPLES

7.021 has 4 s.f.

1st 2nd 3rd 4th

0.003706 has 4 s.f.

1st 2nd 3rd 4th

Take care when rounding that you do not change the place values.

EXAMPLES

Number	to 3 s.f.	to 2 s.f.	to 1 s.f.
4.207	4.21	4.2	4
4379	4380	4400	4000
0.006209	0.00621	0.0062	0.006

After rounding you must fill in the end zeros. For example, 4380 = 4400 to 2 s.f. (not 44). No extra zeros must be put in after the decimal point. For example, 0.013 = 0.01 to 1 s.f. (not 0.010).

Examiner's Top Tip
When rounding to a number of significant figures, remember to retain the size of the number. Example 4380 = 4400 (2 s.f.) – these numbers are approximately the same size.

ROUNDING

QUICK TEST

1. Round 6.493 to 2 decimal places.
2. Round 12.059 to 2 decimal places.
3. Round 9.47 to 1 decimal place.
4. Round 1247 to 2 significant figures.
5. Round 0.00379 to 1 significant figure.
6. Round the following to the nearest 10:

a) 265   b) 7293   c) 1469   d) 25352

1. 6.49 2. 12.06 3. 9.5 4. 1200 5. 0.004 6. a) 270 b) 7290 c) 1470 d) 25350

CHECKING CALCULATIONS

When checking calculations, the process can be reversed like this.

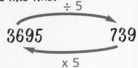

÷ 5

3695   739

x 5

EXAMPLE

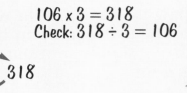

$106 \times 3 = 318$
Check: $318 \div 3 = 106$

x 3

106   318

÷ 3

ESTIMATES AND CHECKING CALCULATIONS

ESTIMATES AND APPROXIMATIONS

LEVEL 7

Estimating is a good way of checking answers.
• Round the numbers to 'easy' numbers, usually 1 or 2 significant figures.
• Work out the estimate using these easy numbers.
• Use the symbol ≈, which means '<u>approximately equal to</u>'.
For multiplying or dividing, never approximate a number with zero.
Use 0.1, 0.01, 0.001, etc.

EXAMPLES
a) $8.93 \times 25.09 \approx 10 \times 25 = 250$
b) $(6.29)^2 \approx 6^2 = 36$
c) $\dfrac{296 \times 52.1}{9.72 \times 1.14} \approx \dfrac{300 \times 50}{10 \times 1} = \dfrac{15000}{10} = 1500$
d) $0.096 \times 79.2 \approx 0.1 \times 80 = 8$

Examiner's Top Tip
Questions which involve approximating are likely to be on the non-calculator paper. Remember to approximate to one significant figure.

EXAMPLE

Jack does the calculation $\dfrac{9.6 \times 103}{(2.9)^2}$

Q
a) Estimate the answer to this calculation, without using a calculator.
b) Jack's answer is 1175.7. Is this the right order of magnitude?

A
a) Estimate $\dfrac{9.6 \times 103}{(2.9)^2} \approx \dfrac{10 \times 100}{3^2} = \dfrac{1000}{9} \approx \dfrac{1000}{10} = 100$

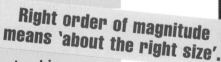

Right order of magnitude means 'about the right size'.

b) Jack's answer is not the right order of magnitude. It is 10 times too big.
When adding and subtracting, very small numbers may be approximated to zero.

EXAMPLES
$109.6 + 0.0002 \approx 110 + 0 = 110$ $63.87 - 0.01 \approx 64 - 0 = 64$

CALCULATIONS

When solving problems the answers should be rounded sensibly.

EXAMPLE
$95.26 \times 6.39 = 608.7114 = 608.71$ (2 d.p.)

Round to 2 d.p. because the values in the question are to 2 d.p.

EXAMPLE
Jackie has £9.37. She divides it equally between 5 people. How much does each person receive?
$£9.37 \div 5 = £1.874$
$ = £1.87$

Round to 1.87 as it is money.

When rounding remainders, consider the context of the question.

EXAMPLE
Paint is sold in 8-litre tins. Sandra needs 27 litres of paint. How many tins must she buy?
$27 \div 8 = 3$ remainder 3
Sandra needs four tins of paint.

Sandra would not have enough paint with three tins, since she is three litres short. Hence the number of tins of paint must be rounded up.

QUICK TEST

Estimate the answers to the following questions.

1. a) $\dfrac{(29.4)^2 + 106}{2.2 \times 5.1}$ b) $\dfrac{294 + 101}{2.1 \times 5.2}$

2. Sukhvinder decided to decorate her living room. The total area of the walls was 48 m². If one roll of wallpaper covers 5 m² of wall, how many rolls of wallpaper will Sukhvinder need?

3. Mr Singh organised a trip to the theatre. 420 students and 10 teachers were going on the trip. If a coach can seat 53 people, how many coaches did he need?

4. Thomas earned £109.25 for working a 23-hour week. How much did he earn per hour? Check your calculation by estimating.

1. a) 100 b) 40   2. 10 rolls of wallpaper.   3. 9 coaches   4. £4.75

BEST BUYS

Unit amounts are looked at to decide
which is the better value for money.

£1.06   £2.81

EXAMPLE

The same brand of breakfast cereal is sold in
two different sized packets.
Which packet represents the better value for money?

- Find the cost per gram for each packet.

  125 g = £1.06   Cost of 1 g = 106 ÷ 125 = 0.848p.
  750 g = £2.81   Cost of 1 g = 281 ÷ 750 = 0.3746p.

- Since the 750 g packet costs less per gram, it is the better value for money.

INCREASING AND DECREASING IN A GIVEN RATIO

- Divide to get one part.
- Multiply for each new part.

EXAMPLE

A photograph of length 9 cm is to be enlarged in the ratio 5 : 3.
What is the length of the enlarged photograph?

- Divide 9 cm by 3 to get one part. 9 ÷ 3 = 3 cm for one part.
- Multiply this by 5. So 5 x 3 = 15 cm on the enlarged
  photograph.

EXAMPLE

A house took 8 people 6 days to build.
At the same rate how long would it take 3 people?
Time for 8 people = 6 days.
Time for 1 person = 8 x 6 = 48 days. It takes one person longer to build the house.
Time for 3 people = $\frac{48}{3}$ = 16 days.   3 people will take $\frac{1}{3}$ of the time taken by
                                                1 person.

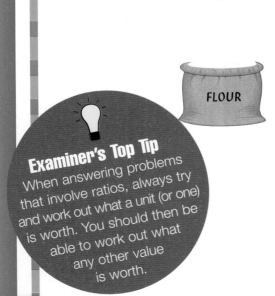

EXAMPLE

A recipe for 4 people needs 1600 g of flour.
How much is needed for 6 people?

- Divide 1600 g by 4, so 400 g for 1 person.
- Multiply by 6, so 6 x 400 g = 2400 g for 6 people.

EXAMPLE

A photocopier is set to reduce in the ratio of 3 : 5.
What is the length of the reduced diagram
if the original is 12 cm?

- Divide 12 by 5 to get 1 part = 2.4 cm.
- Multiply this by 3 to get 3 x 2.4 = 7.2 cm.

SHARING A QUANTITY IN A GIVEN RATIO

- Add up the total parts.
- Work out what one part is worth.
- Work out what the other parts are worth.

EXAMPLE

A forest covers 25 000 hectares. Oak and ash trees are planted in the forest in the ratio 2 : 3. How many hectares do the ash trees cover?

- 2 + 3 = 5 parts
- 5 parts = 25 000 hectares
- 1 part = $\frac{25000}{5}$ = 5000 hectares

Ash has 3 parts, i.e. 3 x 5000
                              = 15 000 hectares.

EXAMPLE

£20 000 is shared in the ratio 1 : 4 between Ewan and Leroy. How much does each receive?

- 1 + 4 = 5 parts
- 5 parts = £20 000
- 1 part = $\frac{25\,000}{5}$ = £4000

So Ewan gets 1 x £4000 = £4000 and Leroy gets 4 x £4000 = £16 000.

> A quick check is to work out the number of hectares the oak trees cover. The total of the oak + ash should be equal to 25 000 hectares.

RATIO

WHAT IS A RATIO?

A ratio is used to compare two or more quantities. '<u>Compared to</u>' is replaced with <u>two dots</u>:
For example, '16 boys compared to 20 girls' can be written as 16 : 20. To simplify ratios, divide both parts of the ratio by the highest factor.
For example, 16 : 20 = 4 : 5 (divide both sides by 4).

EXAMPLES

Simplify the ratio 21 : 28. 21 : 28 = 3 : 4 (divide both sides by 7).
The ratio of red flowers to yellow flowers can be written as:

$10 : 4$
$= \frac{10}{2} : \frac{4}{2}$
$= 5 : 2$

In other words, for every 5 red flowers there are 2 yellow flowers.
To express the ratio 5 : 2 in the ratio <u>n</u> : 1 divide both sides by 2.
$\frac{5}{2} : \frac{2}{2}$
$= 2.5 : 1$

QUICK TEST

1. Write the following ratios in their simplest form:

a) 12 : 15   b) 6 : 12   c) 25 : 10

2. Ahmed and Fiona share £500 between them in the ratio 2 : 3. How much does each receive?

3. A recipe for 12 people uses 500 g of plain flour. How much flour is needed for 18 people?

4. If 15 oranges cost £1.80, how much will 23 identical oranges cost?

5. The same brand of tuna fish is sold in two different sized tins.

   Which tin represents the better value for money?

48 p
TUNA
198 g

76 p
TUNA
240 g

1. a) 4 : 5 b) 1 : 2 c) 5 : 2 2. £200, £300 3. 750 g 4. £2.76 5. Small tin of tuna.

27

1. Write the number 3 248 020 in words.

....

2. Work out the following without a calculator:
   (a) 6214   (b) 6351   (c) 3259   (d) $6\overline{)1290}$
       298 +   2170 –   7 x

....

3. The temperature inside the house is 12°C warmer than outside.
If the temperature outside is –5°C, what is the temperature inside?

....

4. Round these numbers to the nearest 10:
a) 62 b) 55 c) 128 ....
Round these numbers to the nearest 100:
d) 146 e) 289 f) 1350 ....
Round these numbers to the nearest 1000:
g) 7449 h) 8826 ....

5.   1   2   3   4
       5   6   7   8
       9   10   11   12
From the above numbers write down:
a) Any multiples of 3 ....
b) Any prime numbers ....
c) Factors of 20 ....

6. Write 24 as a product of prime factors.

....

7. Work out without a calculator:
a) $\sqrt{100}$ b) 6^2 c) $\sqrt{36}$ d) 2^3

....

8. Jonathan's calculator display shows, 2.76^{09}. Write down what the calculator display means.

....

9. Work out the missing values:
a) $\frac{7}{12} = \frac{14}{X}$ b) $\frac{125}{500} = \frac{y}{100}$ c) $\frac{19}{38} = \frac{76}{Z}$

....

10. A flag is coloured red (27%), blue (61%) and the rest is yellow. What percentage is yellow?

....

11. If an apple costs 18p, work out the cost of 78 similar apples.

....

12. Jessica buys some tins of cat food with a total cost of £8.46. If each tin costs 47p, how many tins does Jessica buy?

....

13. Work out what the missing letters stand for:
a) 12 – A = –3   b) –6 + 10 = B   c) –8 – D = 2   d) 14 + F = –6

....

(c) = **A calculator may be used**   (7) = **This question is for Level 7 students**

14. A jumper costs £45. In a sale it is reduced by 15%; how much does it now cost?

....

15. An orchard has 1600 apple and plum trees divided in the ratio 3 : 5. How many apple trees are in the orchard?

....

16. A house was bought for £75 000. Two years later it was sold for £93 000. Work out the percentage profit.

....

17. A map is being enlarged in the ratio 12 : 7. If the original road length was 21 cm on the map, what is the length of the road on the enlarged map?

....

18. Work out the following:
a) $\frac{2}{9} + \frac{3}{27}$ b) $\frac{3}{5} - \frac{1}{4}$ c) $\frac{6}{9} \times \frac{72}{104}$ d) $\frac{8}{9} \div 1\frac{1}{2}$

....

19. Round the following to two decimal places:
a) 12.693   b) 28.756   c) 2.935

....

20. Round the following to three significant figures:
a) 273 406   b) 0.0007862   c) 27 050

....

21. Complete the table:

Fraction	Decimal	Percentage
....	....	75%
$\frac{2}{5}$	....	....
....	$0.\dot{3}$	....

22. A car was bought for £8995. If the value of the car depreciates by 15% each year, how much will the car be worth after two years?

....

23. Place these values in order, putting the smallest first:
61%   94%   0.93 $\frac{9}{10}$ $\frac{4}{7}$ 0.274

....

24. Without a calculator work out:
a) 6 x 0.001   b) 400 x 0.01   c) 50 ÷ 0.001

....

25. Work these out on your calculator:
a) $\frac{27.1 \times 6.4}{9.3 + 2.7}$ b) $\frac{(9.3)^4}{2.7 \times 3.6}$

....

26. Estimate the answer to $\frac{(29.4)^2 + 106}{2.2 \times 5.1}$

....

How did you do?

1–6	correct	.................start again
7–13	correct	.................getting there
14–20	correct	.................good work
21–26	correct	.................excellent

ALGEBRAIC CONVENTIONS

- <u>Algebra</u> uses letters to represent numbers.
- A <u>term</u> is a collection of numbers, letters and brackets, all multiplied together.
- Terms are separated by + and – signs. Each term has a + or – sign <u>attached</u> <u>to</u> <u>the</u> <u>front</u> <u>of</u> <u>it</u>.

$$3xy - 5r + 2x^2 - 4$$

invisible sign   xy term   r term x^2 term   number term

There are several rules to follow when writing algebra.

$a + a + a + a = 4a$
$b \times b = b^2$ <u>not</u> $2b$
$b \times b \times b = b^3$ <u>not</u> $3b$
$n \times n \times 3 = 3n^2$ <u>not</u> $(3n)^2$
$a \times 3 \times c = 3ac$

Put the number first and then the letters in alphabetical order; leave out the multiplication sign

- When dividing, i.e. $a \div 3$, this is usually written as a fraction, i.e. $\frac{a}{3}$

ALGEBRA 1

WRITING SIMPLE FORMULAE

$n + 4$ is an expression.
$y = n + 4$ is a formula, since it has an = sign in it.

EXAMPLE
A bag of sweets costs 20p. Erin buys some sweets. How much do
(a) 6 bags cost? (b) 10 bags cost?
(c) x bags cost?

(a) $20 \times 6 = 120$ pence.
(b) $20 \times 10 = 200$ pence.
(c) $20 \times x = 20x$ pence.

x can take any value.

In words the above rule can be written as:
Cost of sweets = 20 x number of bags.
This is a <u>formula</u> for working out the cost of any number of bags of sweets. If C represents the cost and b represents the number of bags then:
$C = 20 \times b$
i.e. $C = 20b$; this formula is in <u>symbol</u> <u>form</u>.

Remember to put an equals sign in your formula.

EXAMPLE

number pattern 1   number pattern 2   number pattern 3

a) How many blue tiles will there be in pattern number 4? Drawing the diagram: There are 16 blue tiles.

number pattern 4

b) Write down the formula for finding the number of tiles in pattern number n.
Number of tiles $= 4 \times (n - 1) + 1$
$= 4n + 1$

Make sure an = sign is in the formula.

The 4n is the 4 lots of blue tiles. The +1 is the yellow tile in the middle.

c) How many tiles will be used in pattern number 12?
$n = 12$, i.e. number of tiles $= 4 \times 12 + 1$
$= 48 + 1$
$= 49$

Just substitute the value of n into the formula.

USING LETTERS

EXAMPLE

Emily plants a small vegetable garden. She plants potatoes, carrots and onions. m stands for the number of carrot seeds she has planted.

If she plants five more onion seeds than carrot seeds, how many onion seeds does she plant?

$$m + 5$$ ← This is known as an <u>expression</u>.

If she plants half as many onion seeds as carrot seeds, this is written as $m \div 2$ which is usually written as $\frac{m}{2}$.

> Remember that in algebra a division is usually written as a fraction, i.e.
> $x \div a = \frac{x}{a}$

EXAMPLE

Richard has p counters. David has three times as many counters. Write this as an expression:

    David has $3 \times p$ counters

- $3 \times p$ is written as $3p$ in algebra; the multiplication sign is missed out.

COLLECTING LIKE TERMS

- **Expressions can be simplified by collecting like terms.**
- **Only collect the terms if the letters and powers are identical.**

EXAMPLES

> Remember to put the sign between, i.e. 5a + 2b NOT 5a 2b.

> This minus sign is part of the term 2b.

$$3p + 2p = 5p.$$

$$6a + 2c \text{ cannot be simplified, since there are no like terms.}$$

$$5n + 2n - 6n = n$$ ← Note that n means 1n.

$$2a + 4b + 3a - 2b = 5a + 2b$$ ← Add the a's, then the b's.

$$5xy + 2yx = 7xy \text{ since } xy \text{ is the same as } yx.$$

> **Examiner's Top Tip**
> Algebra forms a large part of the SATS exam. Writing simple formulae like the examples shown in this chapter are very common – practise these types of questions.

QUICK TEST

1.

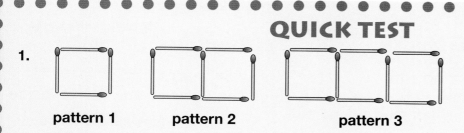

pattern 1   pattern 2   pattern 3

The diagram shows some patterns made up with sticks. If P represents the pattern number and S represents the number of sticks, write down a formula connecting S and P.

2. Write these expressions as simply as possible:

a) 6 more than n   b) 4 less than p   c) 6 more than 3 lots of y

d) h divided by 7   e) 5 less than n divided by p

1. S = 3P + 1 2. a) n + 6 b) p − 4 c) 3y + 6 d) $\frac{h}{7}$ e) $\frac{n}{p}$ − 5

SUBSTITUTING VALUES INTO EXPRESSIONS AND FORMULAE

Replacing a letter with a number is called *substitution*. When substituting:
- write out the expression first, then replace the letters with the values given
- work out the value on your calculator. Use brackets keys where possible and pay attention to <u>order of operations</u>.

EXAMPLES

> Show each step in your working out.

Using $a = 2$, $b = 4.1$, $c = -3$, $d = 5$, find the value of these expressions, giving your answer to 1 decimal place.

a) $\dfrac{a + b}{2}$ b) $\dfrac{a^2 + c^2}{d}$ c) ab d) $3d - ab$

Remember to show the substitution:

> You may need to treat c^2 as $(-3)^2$ depending on your calculator.

a) $\dfrac{a + b}{2} = \dfrac{2 + 4.1}{2} = 3.05 = 3.1$ (1 d.p.)

b) $\dfrac{a^2 + c^2}{d} = \dfrac{2^2 + (-3)^2}{5} = 2.6$

c) $ab = 2 \times 4.1 = 8.2$

> ab means a x b.

d) $3d - ab = (3 \times 5) - (2 \times 4.1) = 6.8$

EXAMPLE

> Work this out carefully on your calculator.

The formula $F = 1.8C + 32$ is used to change temperature in degrees centigrade (C) to temperatures in degrees Fahrenheit (F).

If $C = 20$, work out the value of F.

$F = 1.8C + 32$
$ = 1.8 \times 20 + 32$
$ = 68$

Substitute $C = 20$ into the formula.
Note $1.8C$ means $1.8 \times C$

MULTIPLYING LETTERS AND NUMBERS

- Algebraic expressions are often simplified by multiplying them together, i.e. $5a \times 2b = 10ab$.
- When multiplying expressions, multiply the numbers together, then the letters together.

EXAMPLES

> Multiply the numbers

> Multiply the letters

Simplify these expressions:

a) $3a \times 4b = 3 \times 4 \times a \times b = 12ab$

b) $5a \times 3b \times 2c = 5 \times 3 \times 2 \times a \times b \times c = 30abc$

c) $2a \times 3a = 2 \times 3 \times a \times a = 6a^2$

> Remember $a \times a = a^2$

Examiner's Top Tip
There are a lot of rules/ techniques to learn here. When substituting values in formulae be sure to do it carefully and show full working out.

MULTIPLYING OUT SINGLE BRACKETS

- This helps to simplify algebraic expressions.
- Multiply everything inside the brackets by everything outside the brackets.

EXAMPLES

> This is known as expanding brackets.

$2(a + b) = 2a + 2b$ $3(x - 2) = 3x - 6$

> The multiplication sign is not shown here.

$a(b + d) = ab + ad$ $r(3r - 2s) = 3r^2 - 2rs$

> Remember $r \times r = r^2$

If the term outside the brackets is <u>negative</u>, all of the signs of the terms inside the brackets are <u>changed</u> when multiplying out.

> Remember that $-(a + b)$ means $-1 \times (a + b)$

EXAMPLES

$-2(a + b) = -2a - 2b$ $-a(a - b) = -a^2 + ab$

To simplify expressions, expand the brackets first, then collect like terms.

EXAMPLE

Expand and simplify:

$3(a + 1) + 2(a + b)$ Multiply out brackets.
$3a + 3 + 2a + 2b$ Collect like terms.
$= 5a + 2b + 3$

FACTORISATION (PUTTING BRACKETS IN)

This is the reverse of expanding brackets. An expression is put into brackets by taking out common factors.

$$2(x+4) \xrightarrow{\text{expanding}} 2x + 8$$
$$\xleftarrow{\text{factorising}}$$

EXAMPLES

Factorise:
a) $5x + 10 = 5(x+2)$
b) $8x - 16 = 8(x-2)$
c) $3x + 9 = 3(x+3)$

Remember the highest factor needs to be taken out.

8 is the highest factor of 8 and 16, not 4!

MULTIPLYING OUT TWO BRACKETS

LEVEL 7

Each term in the first bracket is multiplied with each term in the second bracket.

EXAMPLES
Expand and simplify the following:
a) $(x+2)(x+3) = x(x+3) + 2(x+3)$
$= x^2 + 3x + 2x + 6$
$= x^2 + 5x + 6$

b) $(x+4)^2 = (x+4)(x+4)$
$= x(x+4) + 4(x+4)$
$= x^2 + 4x + 4x + 16$
$= x^2 + 8x + 16$

A common error is to think that $(x+4)^2$ means $x^2 + 4^2$ i.e. $x^2 + 16$

REARRANGING A FORMULA

LEVEL 7

The subject of a formula is the letter that appears on its own on one side of the formula. The balancing method can be used to rearrange the formula.

EXAMPLE
Make x the subject of these formulae:
a) $y = \frac{x}{4} + 6$

$y - 6 = \frac{x}{4}$ (subtract 6 from both sides)

$4(y-6) = x$ (multiply both sides by 4)

b) $y = 5(x-2)$

$\frac{y}{5} = (x-2)$ (divide both sides by 5)

$\frac{y}{5} + 2 = x$ (add 2 to both sides)

QUICK TEST

1. Simplify these expressions: a) $5a + 2a + 3a$ b) $6a - 2b + 5b$ c) $3xy + 2yx$
   d) $5a \times 2b$ e) $3a \times 4a$ f) $6a + 2b - 2b + b$

2. Some cards have the following expressions written on them:
   A $2a + 8$ B $2a + 4$ C $4a + 8$ D $4a + 2$
   Which card is the same as $4(a+2)$?

3. If $a = 3$, $b = 2.1$, $c = -4$, work out the answer to these expressions, giving your answer to 1 d.p.
   a) $3a + 2b$ b) $5c - 2a$ c) abc

4. Expand these brackets and simplify   a) $2(x-3)$ b) $(x-2)(x+1)$ c) $(x-1)(x-4)$

5. Factorise: a) $5x - 25$ b) $12x - 20$ c) $4y + 16$

6. Rearrange each formula to make x the subject:
   a) $y = 5x - 2$ b) $y = \frac{3x+4}{7}$ c) $y = \frac{x}{3} + 2$

SOLVING SIMPLE LINEAR EQUATIONS

- An equation involves an unknown value which has to be worked out.
- The balance method is usually used; that is, whatever is done to one side of an equation must be done to the other.

EXAMPLES

Solve the following:

Show all working out and do the calculation step by step.

a) $n - 4 = 6$
$n = 6 + 4$
$n = 10$

Add 4 to both sides.

b) $n + 2 = 8$
$n = 8 - 2$
$n = 6$

Subtract 2 from both sides.

c) $5n = 20$
$n = \frac{20}{5}$
$n = 4$

Divide both sides by 5.

d) $\frac{n}{3} = 2$
$n = 2 \times 3$
$n = 6$

Multiply both sides by 3.

SOLVING EQUATIONS OF THE FORM AX + B = C

EXAMPLES

Solve:

a) $5n + 1 = 11$ ← **Subtract 1 from both sides.**
$5n = 11 - 1$
$5n = 10$
$n = \frac{10}{5} = 2$ ← **Divide both sides by 5.**

b) $\frac{n}{3} + 1 = 4$
$\frac{n}{3} = 4 - 1$
$\frac{n}{3} = 3$
$n = 3 \times 3$ ← **Multiply both sides by 3.**
$n = 9$

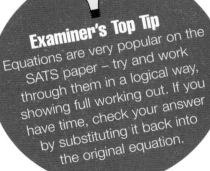

Examiner's Top Tip
Equations are very popular on the SATS paper – try and work through them in a logical way, showing full working out. If you have time, check your answer back into the original equation.

SOLVING LINEAR EQUATIONS OF THE FORM
$AX + B = CX + D$

The trick with this type of equation is to get the X together on one side of the equals sign and the numbers on the other side.

EXAMPLE
Solve:

$7X - 2 = 2X + 13$

$7X - 2 - 2X = 13$

$5X = 13 + 2$

$5X = 15$

$X = \frac{15}{5} = 3$

**Subtract 2X from both sides.
Add 2 to both sides**

EQUATIONS ①

SOLVING LINEAR EQUATIONS WITH BRACKETS

Just because an equation has brackets don't be put off – it's just the same as the other equations once the brackets have been multiplied out.

EXAMPLE

$5(2X - 1) = 10$

$10X - 5 = 10$

$10X = 10 + 5$

$10X = 15$

$X = \frac{15}{10} = 1.5$

Multiply brackets out first.

$4(2n + 5) = 3(n + 10)$

$8n + 20 = 3n + 30$

$8n + 20 - 3n = 30$

$5n = 30 - 20$

$5n = 10$

$n = \frac{10}{5} = 2$

Multiply brackets out first.

Solve as before.

QUICK TEST

Solve the following equations:

1. $2X = 10$

2. $2X - 3 = 9$

3. $4X + 1 = 8$

4. $5X + 3 = 2X + 9$

5. $6X - 1 = 2X + 15$

6. $3(X + 2) = X + 4$

7. $2(X - 1) = 6(2X + 2)$

1. $x=5$ 2. $x=6$ 3. $x=\frac{7}{4}$ 4. $x=2$ 5. $x=4$ 6. $x=-1$ 7. $x=-1.4$

EQUATIONS 2

SIMULTANEOUS EQUATIONS

Two equations with two unknowns are called <u>simultaneous equations</u>.

They can be solved in several ways. Solving equations simultaneously involves finding values for the letters that will make both equations work.

GRAPHICAL METHOD
The points at which any two graphs intersect represent the simultaneous solutions of these equations.

EXAMPLE
Solve the simultaneous equations:
$y = 2x - 3$, $y - x = 1$ by a graphical method.

* Draw the two graphs:
  $y = 2x - 3$ If $x = 0$, $y = -3$
  If $y = 0$, $x = \frac{3}{2}$
  $y - x = 1$ If $x = 0$, $y = 1$
  If $y = 0$, $x = -1$

* At the point of intersection
  $x = 4$ and $y = 5$.

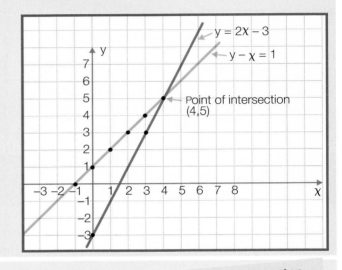

ELIMINATION METHOD
* If the coefficient of one of the letters is the same in both equations, then that letter may be eliminated by subtracting the equations.

> Work out the coordinates for when $x = 0$ and $y = 0$ to draw a quick graph.

> The <u>coefficient</u> is the number a letter is multiplied by, e.g. the coefficient of $-3x$ is -3.

EXAMPLE
Solve simultaneously $n + 3p = 25$, $2n + p = 15$.

$n + 3p = 25$	1	Label the equations 1 and 2.
$2n + p = 15$	2	As no coefficients match, multiply equation 2 by 3.
$6n + 3p = 45$	3	The coefficients are now the same in equations 1 and 3.
$5n + 0p = 20$		Subtract equation 1 from equation 3.

So $5n = 20$,
i.e. $\underline{n = 4}$.

$2n + p = 15$ Substitute the value of $n = 4$ into equation 1 or 2.
so $8 + p = 15$,
i.e. $\underline{p = 7}$.

Check in equation 1 $4 + 3 \times 7 = 25$ ✓
(Substitute $n = 4$ and $p = 7$ into the other equation.)
The solution is $n = 4$ and $p = 7$.

> Always check that the values work.

To eliminate terms with <u>opposite</u> signs <u>add</u>.
To eliminate terms with <u>the same</u> signs <u>subtract</u>.

Examiner's Top Tip
Simultaneous equations are usually a difficult topic to master. Try and learn the steps outlined above and practise lots of examples. Use the check at the end to make sure you have got the answer right.

USING EQUATIONS TO SOLVE PROBLEMS

EXAMPLE

Class 9A were playing a number game. Saima said 'Multiplying my number by 5 and adding 8 gives the same answer as subtracting my number from 20.'

a) Call Saima's number y and form an equation.
$5y + 8 = 20 - y$

b) Solve the equation to work out Saima's number:
$5y + 8 = 20 - y$
$5y + 8 + y = 20$
$6y = 20 - 8$
$6y = 12$
$y = \frac{12}{6} = 2$ Saima's number is 2.

> Check at the end that $y = 2$ works in the equation.

EXAMPLE

The lengths of the triangle are given in the diagram opposite.

a) Write down an expression for the perimeter of the triangle, if the perimeter of the triangle is 39 cm.

b) Form an equation and solve it to find the length of each side.

$x + 2$ $2x + 4$ $3x - 3$

a) Perimeter $= (x + 2) + (3x - 3) + (2x + 4)$
$= 6x + 3$

b) $6x + 3 = 39$
$6x = 39 - 3$
$6x = 36$
$x = \frac{36}{6}$
$\therefore x = 6$

> The perimeter is found by adding the three lengths.

Each length is $x + 2 = 8$ cm
$2x + 4 = 16$ cm
$3x - 3 = 15$ cm

LEVEL 7

QUICK TEST

1. Solve the following pairs of simultaneous equations:

a) $4x + 7y = 10$
   $2x + 3y = 3$

b) $3a - 5b = 1$
   $2a + 3b = 7$

2. a) Write down an equation for the perimeter of the rectangle opposite, if the perimeter is 74 cm.

   b) Solve the equation to find the length and width of the rectangle.

$5x + 4$

$x - 3$

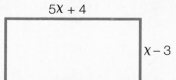

1. a) $x = -4.5$ b) $a = 2$ 2. a) $12x + 2 = 74$ b) $x = 6$ $\therefore$ length = 34
   $y = 4$ $b = 1$ width = 3

37

SOLVING CUBIC EQUATIONS BY TRIAL AND IMPROVEMENT

This is when successive approximations are made in order to get closer to the correct value.

EXAMPLE

The equation $x^3 - 5x = 10$ has a solution between 2 and 3. Find this solution to two decimal places.

> Make sure you write down the solution of x, not the answer to $x^3 - 5x$.

Draw a table to help.

Substitute different values of x into $x^3 - 5x$.

x	$x^3 - 5x$	Comment
2.5	3.125	too small
2.8	7.952	too small
2.9	9.889	too small
2.95	10.922375	too big
2.94	10.712184	too big
2.91	10.092171	too big

At this stage the solution is trapped between 2.90 and 2.91. Checking the middle value $x = 2.905$ gives $x^3 - 5x = 9.99036 \ldots$ which is too small.

```
   2.90           2.905           2.91
(too small)    (too small)     (too big)
```

The diagram makes it clear that the solution is 2.91 correct to two decimal places.

Examiner's Top Tip
- When solving equations by trial and improvement it is the value of x which is needed as the solution.
- Remember to solve inequalities in a similar way to equations.

INEQUALITIES

LEVEL 7

These are expressions where one side is not equal to the other. Inequalities are solved in a similar way to equations.

$\geq$ means 'greater than or equal to' $>$ means 'greater than'
$\leq$ means 'less than or equal to' $<$ means 'less than'

So $x > 3$ and $3 < x$ both say 'x is greater than 3'.

- Inequalities are solved in a similar way to equations.
- Multiplying and dividing by negative numbers changes the direction of the sign.
  For example, if $-x \geq 3$ then $x \leq -3$.

EXAMPLE

a) Solve the following inequality:

$5x - 1 < 3x + 5$
$2x - 1 < 5$ Subtract $3x$ from both sides.
$2x < 6$ Add 1 to both sides.
$x < 3$ Divide both sides by 2.

> Use the same method that you used when solving equations.

The solution of the inequality may be represented on a number line.

> Use • when the end point is included and ○ when the end point is not included.

b) Solve the following inequality:

$-5 < 3x + 1 \leq 13$ Subtract 1 from each side.
$-6 < 3x \leq 12$ Divide by 3.
$-2 < x \leq 4$

On a number line the solution of the inequality looks like

The integer values (whole numbers) which satisfy the above inequality are $-1, 0, 1, 2, 3, 4$.

TRIAL AND IMPROVEMENT AND INEQUALITIES

QUICK TEST

C 1. If $12x - x^2 = 34$ has a solution between 4 and 5, use trial and improvement to find the value of x to 1 decimal place.

2. Solve the following inequalities:

a) $2x - 3 < 9$

b) $5x + 1 \geq 21$

c) $1 \leq 3x - 2 \leq 7$

d) $1 \leq 5x + 2 < 12$

NUMBER PATTERNS AND SEQUENCES

A sequence is a list of numbers. There is usually a relationship between the numbers. Each value in the list is called a <u>term</u>.

- There are lots of different number patterns. When finding a missing number in the number pattern it is sensible to see what is happening in the gap.

EXAMPLES
The odd numbers have <u>a common difference</u> of two:

The rule is add 2 each time.

1   3   5   7   9, . . .
   2   2   2   2

The next term in this sequence is found by multiplying the previous term by 3:

2,   6,   18,   54, . . .
  x3   x3   x3

The next term in this sequence is found by adding the two previous terms:

1,   1,   2,   3,   5,   8,   13
1 + 1   2 + 3   5 + 8

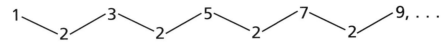

NUMBER PATTERNS AND SEQUENCES

DIVIDING BY 2, 5 AND 10

One number is <u>divisible</u> by another if there is no remainder.

EXAMPLE
4 is divisible by 2,

$4 \div 2 = 2$

7 is not divisible by 2,

$7 \div 2 = 3.5$

- A number is divisible by 2 if it is an even number.
- A number is divisible by 5 if it ends in 0 or 5.
- A number is divisible by 10 if it ends in 0.

FINDING THE NTH TERM OF A LINEAR SEQUENCE

- The nth term is often shown as U_n, e.g. the 12th term is U_{12}.
- For a linear sequence the nth term takes the form of $U_n = an + b$.

The gap or difference gives the value of a.

EXAMPLE
Find the nth term of this sequence:
4, 7, 10, 13, 16
- Look at the difference between the terms. If they are the same this gives the <u>multiple</u> or <u>a</u>.

- Adjust the rule by adding or taking away.

term	1	2	3	4	5	. . . n
sequence	4	7	10	13	16	
	3	3	3	3	

Check your rule with the second term to make sure it works.

The multiple is 3, i.e. 3n.
If n is 1, 3 × 1 = 3 but we need 4 so add 1.
nth term $\underline{U_n = 3n + 1}$.

COMMON NUMBER PATTERNS

These number patterns are common and need to be remembered.

1, 4, 9, 16, 25, . . .	Square numbers
1, 8, 27, 64, 125, . . .	Cube numbers
1, 3, 6, 10, 15, . . .	Triangular numbers
1, 1, 2, 3, 5, 8, 13, . . .	Fibonacci sequence
2, 4, 8, 16, 32, 64, . . .	Powers of 2
10, 100, 1000, 10 000, 100 000, . . .	Powers of 10

FINDING THE NTH TERM OF A QUADRATIC SEQUENCE

For a quadratic sequence the first differences are not constant but the second differences are.

The nth term takes the form of $U_n = an^2 + bn + c$, where b and c may be zero.

LEVEL 7

EXAMPLE

For the sequence of square numbers find an expression for the nth term.

First difference
Second difference

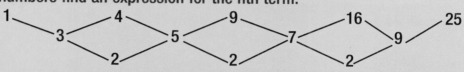

- Since the second differences are the same, the rule for the nth term is quadratic.

- The nth term is n^2.

EXAMPLE

Find the nth term of this sequence.

First difference
Second difference

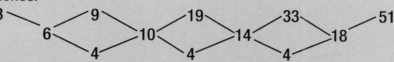

- Since the second differences are the same then the rule for the nth term is quadratic.

- The coefficient of n^2 is $\frac{\text{(second difference)}}{2}$ i.e. $4 \div 2 = 2$

- Adjusting as before gives $2n^2 + 1$

Examiner's Top Tip
Finding the nth term is a very useful method since it helps you to find a formula when given a sequence of values.
You must take care though when finding the nth term of a quadratic sequence since they are more difficult.

• •

QUICK TEST

Find the nth term of each of these sequences:

1. a) 5, 7, 9, 11, 13

b) 3, 7, 11, 15, 19

c) 8, 11, 14, 17, 20

d) 2, 5, 10, 17, 26

2. Find the next two numbers in this sequence:

32, 16, 8, 4,__, __,

1. a) 2n + 3 b) 4n − 1 c) 3n + 5 d) n² + 1 2. 2, 1

COORDINATES

- Coordinates are used to locate the position of a point.
- When reading coordinates, read across first, then up or down.
- Coordinates are always written with <u>brackets</u>, and a <u>comma</u> in between, i.e. (2, 4).
- The horizontal axis is the <u>x</u> axis. The vertical axis is the <u>y</u> axis.

EXAMPLES

A has coordinates (2, 4)
B has coordinates (−1, 3)
C has coordinates (−2, −3)
D has coordinates (3, −1)

Make sure you write the brackets and comma.

Remember to read across first, then up or down.

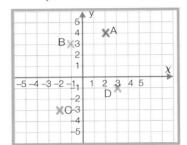

FUNCTION MACHINES

EXAMPLE

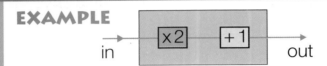

in → x2 → +1 → out

When the numbers are fed into this function machine, they are first multiplied by 2 and then added to 1.

If 1 is fed in, 3 comes out (i.e. 1 x 2 + 1 = 3)
If 2 is fed in, 5 comes out (i.e. 2 x 2 + 1 = 5)
If 3 is fed in, 7 comes out (i.e. 3 x 2 + 1 = 7)
If 4 is fed in, 9 comes out (i.e. 4 x 2 + 1 = 9)
This transformation can be illustrated with a <u>mapping diagram</u>, like this:

1 ⇨ 3
2 ⇨ 5
3 ⇨ 7
4 ⇨ 9

To describe the mapping, $x ⇨ 2x + 1$ is written. This is read 'x becomes $2x + 1$'.

Examiner's Top Tip

To work out the coordinates for the graph you can either:
- draw up a table as shown in the examples, or
- use a function machine or mapping diagrams.

Once the coordinates are plotted, check they are on a straight line. If not, go back and check the coordinates have been worked out properly.

GRAPH DRAWING

- Coordinates are used to draw graphs.
- Before a graph can be drawn the coordinates need to be worked out.

FINDING THE GRADIENT OF A STRAIGHT LINE

- **To find the gradient, choose two points.**
- **Draw a triangle as shown.**
- **Find the change in y (height) and the change in x (base).**
- **Gradient = $\frac{change\ in\ y}{change\ in\ x}$ or $\frac{height}{base} = \frac{4}{3} = 1\frac{1}{3}$**
- **Decide if the gradient is positive or negative.**

Do not count the squares as the scales may be different.

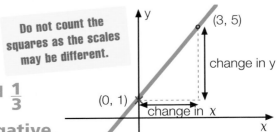

GRAPHS OF THE FORM Y = MX + C

These are straight line (linear) graphs.
The general equation of a straight line graph is $y = mx + c$.
<u>m</u> is the <u>gradient</u> (steepness) of the line.
<u>c</u> is the <u>intercept</u> on the y axis, that is, where the graph cuts the y axis.
<u>Parallel</u> lines have the same <u>gradient</u>.

Putting the coordinates in a table makes it easier.

EXAMPLE

Draw the graphs of $y = 2x$, $y = -2x$, $y = 3x$ and $y = x - 2$ on the same axes.

- Work out coordinates for each graph.

$y = 2x$

x	-2	-1	0	1	2
y	-4	-2	0	2	4

$y = 3x$

x	-2	-1	0	1	2
y	-6	-3	0	3	6

$y = -2x$

x	-2	-1	0	1	2
y	4	2	0	-2	-4

$y = x - 2$

x	-2	-1	0	1	2
y	-4	-3	-2	-1	0

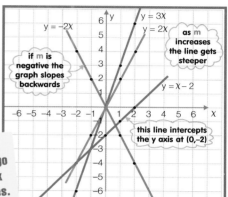

if m is negative the graph slopes backwards

as m increases the line gets steeper

this line intercepts the y axis at (0,–2)

- Plot each set of coordinates and join up the points with a straight line.
- Label each of the graphs.

If your line is not straight, go back and check your coordinates.

COORDINATES AND GRAPHS

QUICK TEST

1. What are the coordinates of the points A, B, C, D, E and F?

2. The graph of $y = x - 1$ is drawn on the graph opposite. Draw the following graphs on the same axes.

a) $y = 2x$

b) $y = 4x$

c) What do you notice about the graphs of $y = 2x$ and $y = 4x$?

d) Without working out any coordinates draw the graph of $y = x - 2$.

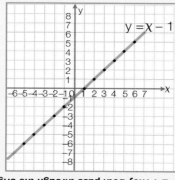

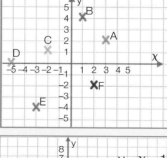

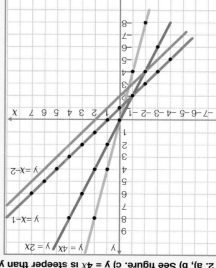

1. A = (3, 2) B = (1, 4) C = (−2, 1) D = (−5, 0) E = (−3, −4) F = (2, −2)
2. a), b) See figure. c) y = 4x is steeper than y = 2x. They both pass through the origin. d) See figure.

MORE GRAPHS

GRAPHS OF THE FORM Y = Ax² + B

- These are curved graphs.

EXAMPLE
Draw the graph of $y = x^2 - 2$

x	−3	−2	−1	0	1	2	3
y	7	2	−1	−2	−1	2	7

- Work out the y coordinates for each point.

- Remember that x^2 means x times x.

- Just replace x in the equation with each coordinate, i.e. $x = -3$ so $y = (-3)^2 - 2 = 7$.

- The table represents the coordinates of the graph. The coordinates can now be plotted to form the graph.

- Join up the points with a smooth curve and label the graph.

- If you were asked to draw the graph of $y = 2x^2$

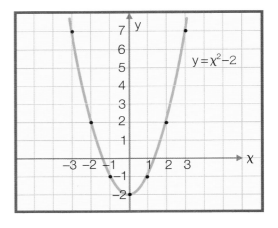

Use a calculator to help work out the coordinates.

Try and join the points with a smooth curve.

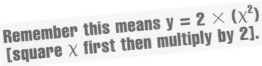

Remember this means $y = 2 \times (x^2)$ [square x first then multiply by 2].

DIRECTION OF THE CURVE
If the number in front of x^2 is positive the curve looks like this:

If the number in front of x^2 is negative the curve looks like this:

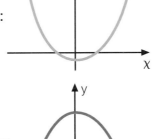

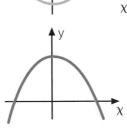

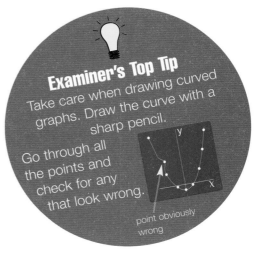

Examiner's Top Tip
Take care when drawing curved graphs. Draw the curve with a sharp pencil.

Go through all the points and check for any that look wrong.

point obviously wrong

GRAPHS OF THE FORM Y = A, X = B

EXAMPLE

Draw the line y = 3. Draw the line x = 2.

y = a is a __horizontal line__ with every y coordinate equal to a.

x = b is a __vertical line__ with every x coordinate equal to b.

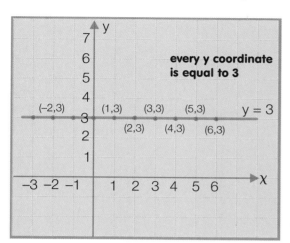

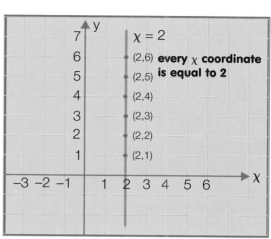

THE GRAPH OF Y = X^3

When asked to draw the graph of y = x^3, follow the methods as shown before.

Remember $x^3 = x \times x \times x$

- Work out the y coordinate for each point.
- Replace x in the equation with the coordinate.

x	−3	−2	−1	0	1	2	3
y	−27	−8	−1	0	1	8	27

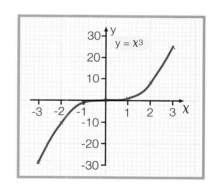

- Plot the x and y coordinates from the table above.
- Notice the shape of the graph of y = x^3.

QUICK TEST

1. Draw the graph of y = $2x^2 + 1$

   for values of x from −3 to 3.

   Complete the table of values

x	−3	−2	−1	0	1	2	3
y	19						

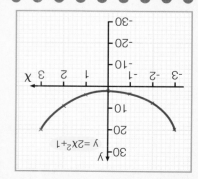

GRAPHS IN PRACTICAL SITUATIONS

CONVERSION GRAPHS

- These are used to convert one measurement into another measurement.

EXAMPLE

£1 = 200 pesetas.
- To change £3.50 into pesetas, read up to the line and then across, i.e. 700 pesetas.
- To change 500 pesetas, read across to the line and then read down, i.e. £2.50.

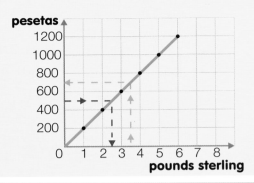

DISTANCE–TIME GRAPHS

These are often known as travel graphs.
Distance is on the vertical axis; time is on the horizontal axis.
The speed of an object can be found from a distance–time graph by using:

$$\text{speed} = \frac{\text{distance travelled}}{\text{time taken}}$$

EXAMPLE

The graph shows Mr Roger's car journey.
Work out his speed at each stage of the journey.

(a) For the first stage of the journey:

$$\text{speed} = \frac{\text{distance}}{\text{time}} = \frac{30}{1} = 30 \text{ m.p.h.}$$

So the car travels at 30 m.p.h. for 1 hour.

(b) The car is stationary for 30 minutes.

(c) The graph is steeper so the car is travelling faster.

$$\text{speed} = \frac{\text{distance}}{\text{time}} = \frac{30}{0.5} = 60 \text{ m.p.h.}$$

(d) The car is stationary for 1 hour.

(e) For the return journey the speed is

$$\text{speed} = \frac{\text{distance}}{\text{time}} = \frac{60}{1.5} = 40 \text{ m.p.h.}$$

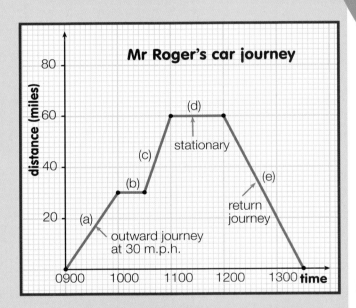

Always check you understand the graph's scales before starting a question.

Remember 30 minutes is 0.5 hours.

USING LINEAR GRAPHS

- Linear graphs are often used to show relationships.

EXAMPLES

The graph shows the charges made by a van hire firm.

- Point A shows how much was charged for hiring the van, i.e. £50.

- The gradient shows that £20 was then charged per day. Hence for 5 days' hire, the van cost £50 + £20 x 5 = £150.

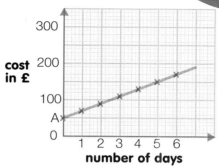

Examiner's Top Tip
All these graphs are useful for looking at linear relationships. It is useful to draw any lines on your graph to help show how you obtained your answers.

USING LINEAR GRAPHS

Key points

When answering questions involving distance–time graphs try and keep the following in mind.

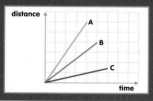

The steeper the graph the greater the speed.
Object A is travelling faster than object B which in turn is travelling faster than object C

The green line shows an incorrect journey home because you cannot go back in time!

QUICK TEST

The distance–time graph shows Mrs Roberts' car journey.

a) What speed did she travel at for the first 2 hours?

b) What is Mrs Roberts doing at A?

c) At what speed is her return journey?

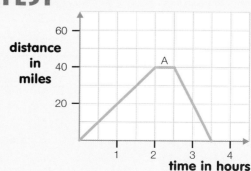

a) 20 m.p.h.   b) Staying stationary   c) 40 m.p.h.

47

EXAM-STYLE QUESTIONS —

1. Write these expressions as simply as possible:
a) 5 more than r ....b) 7 less than y ....
c) p divided by 4 ....d) 4 less than r, divided by s ....

2. Simplify these expressions:
a) 5a + 2a + 3a ....b) 6a – 2b + 5b ....
c) 3Xy + 2yX ....d) 5a x 2b.......................................
e) 3a x 4a..f) 6a + 2b – 2b + b...............................

3. A shape has the lengths shown in the diagram. Write down an expression for the perimeter of the shape.

4b   3a
5a
5
6b

....

4. Here is a pattern made up of regular hexagons of side length 1 cm.
a) Here is a table showing the pattern number and perimeter of the shapes. Complete this table:

(1)   (2)   (3)   (4)

Pattern number (n)	1	2	3	4	5	6
Perimeter of shape (p)	6		14			

b) Write down a formula that connects the perimeter (p) and the pattern number (n).

....

5. If a = 3, b = 2 and c = –1, calculate the value of each of the following:
a) a + b + c ....
b) 2a – 3b ....
c) 5a – 2c ....
d) $a^2 + c^2 – 2b$ ....

6. Using the formula v = u + at:
a) Calculate v when u = 200, a = 30 t = 4 ....
b) Calculate v when u = 500, a = 40 t = 10 ....

7. Some cards have the following expressions on them:

| 2n + 8 | n^2 | 2n + 4 | 2n | 5n | 4n + 8 | 2n – 2 | 4n + 2 | 2n – 1 | n + n |

Which cards are the same as:
a) 4(n + 2) ....
b) n x n ....
c) 2(n – 1) ....
d) 2n + 2n – 3 + 5 ....

8. Solve the following equations:
a) n – 6 = 10 ....
b) 2n = 12 ....
c) 5a + 10 = 15 ....
d) $\frac{n}{5}$ – 1 = 6 ....

9. The graph of y = X – 2 is drawn on the graph opposite.
Draw the following graphs on the same axes:
a) y = 2X   b) y = 3X
c) What do you notice about the graphs of y = 2X and y = 3X?

....

d) Without working out any coordinates, draw the graph of y = 2X – 4.

C = A calculator may be used   **7** = This question is for Level 7 students

10. Solve the following equations:
a) $6n + 2 = 4n + 8$ ....
b) $6(n + 2) = 5n + 7$ ....
c) $2(n - 1) = 3(n + 4)$ ....

11. A rectangle has a length of $(2n + 1)$ cm and a width of 4 cm.
a) Write an expression for the perimeter of the rectangle. Simplify as much as possible.

4 cm | (2n+1) cm

....

b) If the perimeter of the rectangle is 22 cm, write an equation involving n and solve it to find the value of n.

....

12. Write down the nth term of the following sequence:
5, 7, 9, 11, 13, ...
....

13. Factorise the following expressions:
a) $5X + 15$ ....
b) $6X - 12$ ....
c) $12X + 20$ ....

14. For each function write down the gradient and intercept of each of these lines:
a) $y = 4X + 10$ ....
b) $y = 6 - 2X$ ....

15. The travel graph shows the car journeys of two people.
From the travel graph find:
a) the speed at which Miss Young is travelling
b) the length of time Mr Price has a break
c) the speed of Mr Price from London to Birmingham
d) the time at which Miss Young and Mr Price pass each other.

distance (miles)

London 200

Birmingham 100

Manchester

Miss Young

Mr Price

1300 1400 1500 1600 1700 1800

time

LEVEL 7
16. Solve these simultaneous equations:
$2X + 3y = 6$
$X + y = 1$

17. Solve these inequalities and represent the solution on a number line:
a) $3n + 2 < 6$ ....
b) $5n - 1 \leq 2n + 5$ ....

LEVEL 7
18. Write down the nth term of this sequence:
3, 6, 11, 18, ...
....

LEVEL 7
19. Rearrange the formula to make x the subject:
$y = \dfrac{X}{3} - 6$
....
....

How did you do?

1–4	correct	....start again
5–10	correct	....getting there
11–15	correct	....good work
16–19	correct	....excellent

POLYGONS

These are 2D shapes with straight sides. Regular polygons are shapes with all sides and angles equal.

Number of sides	Name of polygon
3	Triangle
4	Quadrilateral
5	Pentagon
6	Hexagon
7	Heptagon
8	Octagon

REGULAR PENTAGON
- five equal sides
- rotational symmetry of order 5
- five lines of symmetry

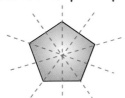

REGULAR HEXAGON
- six equal sides
- rotational symmetry of order 6
- six lines of symmetry

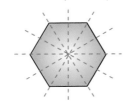

REGULAR OCTAGON
- eight equal sides
- rotational symmetry of order 8
- eight lines of symmetry

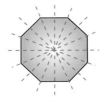

QUADRILATERALS

You need to be able to sketch these shapes and know their symmetrical properties.

These are four-sided shapes.

SQUARE
Four lines of symmetry
Rotational symmetry of order 4

RECTANGLE
Two lines of symmetry
Rotational symmetry of order 2

PARALLELOGRAM
No lines of symmetry
Rotational symmetry of order 2

RHOMBUS
Two lines of symmetry
Rotational symmetry of order 2

Parallel lines are lines that remain the same distance apart, i.e. they never meet.

KITE
One line of symmetry
No rotational symmetry

TRAPEZIUM
Isosceles trapezium:
One line of symmetry
No rotational symmetry

isoseles trapezium

No lines of symmetry
No rotational symmetry

trapezium

TRIANGLES

There are several types of triangles.

RIGHT ANGLED
Has a 90° angle.

EQUILATERAL
Three sides equal.
Three angles equal.

ISOSCELES
Two sides equal.
Base angles equal.

SCALENE
No sides or
angles the same.

SHAPES

Examiner's Top Tip
Try and learn all the shapes and their symmetrical properties.

THE CIRCLE

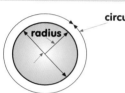

circumference

radius

chord

arc

tangent

o

o

perpendicular bisector

radius

tangent

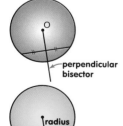

Diameter = 2 x radius.

The <u>circumference</u> is the distance around the outside edge.

A <u>chord</u> is a line that joins two points on the circumference. The line does not go through the centre.
A <u>tangent</u> touches the circle at one point only.
An <u>arc</u> is part of the circumference.

An angle in a semicircle is always a <u>right</u> <u>angle</u>.

The <u>perpendicular</u> <u>bisector</u> of a chord passes through the centre of a circle.

The radius and tangent at a point make an angle of 90°.

QUICK TEST

1. What is the name of a six-sided polygon?

2. From memory draw all the main triangles and quadrilaterals.

3D SHAPES

A prism is a solid that can be cut into slices which are all the same shape.

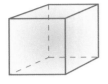
cube

cuboid

sphere

cylinder

cone

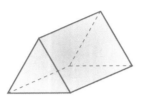
triangular prism

square-based pyramid

Examiner's Top Tip
Remember to learn the mathematical names of the solids. When drawing nets accurately, make sure that you are careful when measuring the sides.

NETS OF SOLIDS

The net of a 3D shape is a 2D (flat) shape, which is <u>folded</u> to make the 3D shape.

EXAMPLES

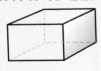
cuboid

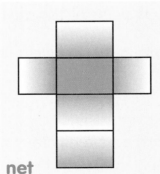
net

When asked to draw an accurate net, you must measure carefully.

triangular prism

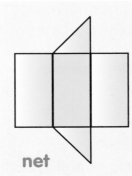
net

When making the shape, remember to put tabs on, to stick it together.

FACES, EDGES AND VERTICES

A <u>face</u> is a flat surface of a solid.
An <u>edge</u> is where two faces meet.
<u>Vertex</u> is another word for a corner.
The plural is <u>vertices</u>.
The cuboid has six faces,
eight vertices and 12 edges.

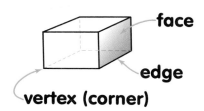

face
edge
vertex (corner)

Edges which cannot be seen are usually shown with a dotted line.

SOLIDS

PLANS AND ELEVATIONS

A <u>plan</u> is what is seen if a 3D shape is looked down on from above.
An <u>elevation</u> is seen if the 3D shape is looked at from the side or front.

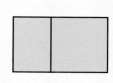

A

B

C

plan A

front elevation B

side elevation C

QUICK TEST

1. Draw an accurate net of this 3D shape.

5.7cm
4 cm
4 cm
4 cm

2. Draw a sketch of the plan and elevations from A and B of this solid.

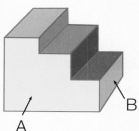

A

B

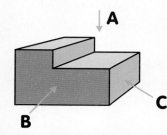

1.
5.7cm
5.7cm
5.7 cm
5.7cm
4cm
4cm
4cm
4cm
4 cm

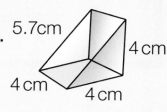

plan

side elevation
B

view from A
(front elevation)

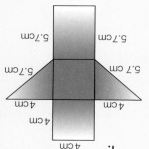 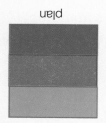 

2.

53

SYMMETRY

REFLECTIVE SYMMETRY

- Both sides of a shape are symmetrical when a mirror line is drawn across it. The mirror line is known as the <u>line</u> or <u>axis of symmetry</u>.

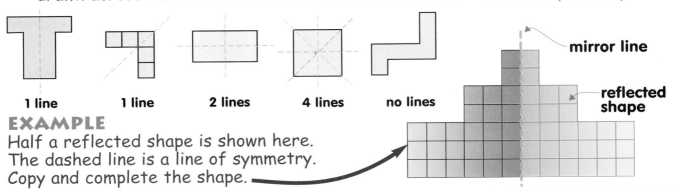

1 line **1 line** **2 lines** **4 lines** **no lines**

mirror line

reflected shape

EXAMPLE

Half a reflected shape is shown here. The dashed line is a line of symmetry. Copy and complete the shape.

ROTATIONAL SYMMETRY

- A 2D (two-dimensional) shape has rotational symmetry, if when it is turned, it looks exactly the same. The <u>order of rotational symmetry</u> is the number of times the shape turns and looks the same.

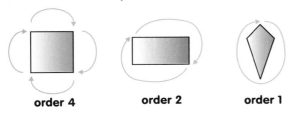

order 4   **order 2**   **order 1**

For the kite the shape has one position. It is said to have <u>rotational symmetry of order 1</u> or <u>no</u> rotational symmetry.

PLANE SYMMETRY

This is symmetry in 3D (three-dimensional) solids only.

A 3D shape has a plane of symmetry if the plane divides the shape into two halves, and one half is the exact mirror image of the other.

plane of symmetry

QUICK TEST

1. The dotted lines are the lines of symmetry.
   Complete the shape so that it is symmetrical.

2. What are the names of the three types of symmetry?

3. Draw a plane of symmetry on this solid.

1.   **3.**

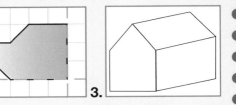

3. reflective, rotational, Plane .2   :9-E.1.1

54

CONSTRUCTING A TRIANGLE

EXAMPLE
Use compasses to construct this triangle.
- Draw the longest side.
- With the compass point at A, draw an arc of radius 4 cm.
- With the compass point at B, draw an arc of radius 5 cm.
- Join A and B to the point where the two arcs meet at C.

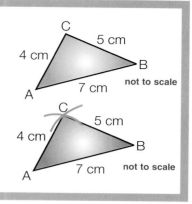

BISECTING AN ANGLE

- Draw two lines XY and YZ to meet at an angle.
- Using compasses, place the point at Y and draw the two arcs on XY and YZ.
- Place the compass points at the two arcs on XY and YZ and draw arcs to cross at N. Join Y to N. YN is the <u>bisector</u> of angle XYZ.

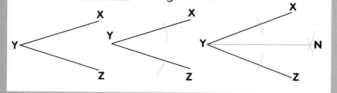

LOGO
- This is a computer program which is used to draw shapes.
- Transformations can take place using LOGO.

EXAMPLE
Shape Y is an equilateral triangle. The instructions to draw shape Y are:

FORWARD 4
TURN RIGHT 120°
FORWARD 4
TURN RIGHT 120°
FORWARD 4

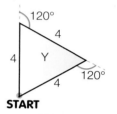

CONSTRUCTIONS AND LOGO

Examiner's Top Tip
Constructions are useful when answering locus questions and questions on scale drawings.

PERPENDICULAR BISECTOR OF A LINE

- Draw a line XY.
- Draw two arcs with the compasses, using X as the centre. The compasses must be set at a radius greater than half the distance of XY.
- Draw two more arcs with Y as the centre (keep the compasses the same distance apart as before).
- Join the two points where the arcs cross.
- AB is the **perpendicular** **bisector** of XY.
- N is the **midpoint** of XY.

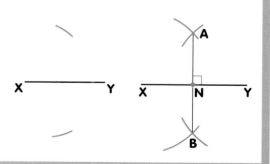

QUICK TEST

1. Shape A is a rectangle. Complete the LOGO commands for drawing the rectangle:

FORWARD 2
TURN RIGHT 90°
FORWARD 5

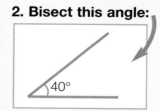

2. Bisect this angle:

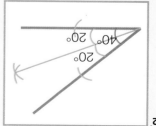

ANGLES AND THE PROTRACTOR

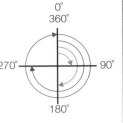

An angle is an amount of turning or rotation. Angles are measured using a protractor, in degrees. A circle is divided into 360 parts. Each part is called a degree and is represented by a small circle °.

An <u>acute</u> angle is between 0° and 90°.

An <u>obtuse</u> angle is between 90° and 180°.

A <u>reflex</u> angle is between 180° and 360°.

A <u>right angle</u> is 90°.

MEASURING ANGLES USING A PROTRACTOR

A protractor is used to measure the size of an angle.

Beware, make sure you put the 0° line at the start position and read from the correct scale.

When measuring angles, count the degree lines carefully and always double check.

Read from 0° on the outer scale.

For the above angle measure on the outer scale since you must start from 0°.

150°

Place the cross at the point of the angle you are measuring.

ANGLES IN PARALLEL LINES

<u>Alternate</u> (Z) angles are <u>equal</u>.

<u>Corresponding</u> angles are <u>equal</u>.

<u>Supplementary</u> angles add up to <u>180°</u>
c + d = <u>180°</u>.

READING ANGLES

When asked to find ABC or ∠ABC or AB̂C, find the angle shown by the <u>middle letter</u>, in this case B.

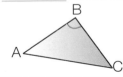

TESSELLATIONS

- A tessellation is a pattern of 2D shapes which fit together without leaving any gaps.
- For shapes to tessellate, the angles at each point must add up to 360°.

EXAMPLE

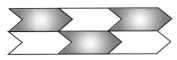

Examiner's Top Tip
Always make sure that you show full working out when carrying out an angle calculation.

ANGLE FACTS

Angles on a <u>straight line</u> add up to <u>180°</u>
$a + b + c = 180°$

Angles at a <u>point</u> add up to <u>360°</u>
$a + b + c = 360°$

Angles in a <u>triangle</u> add up to <u>180°</u>
$a + b + c = 180°$

Angles in a <u>quadrilateral</u> add up to <u>360°</u>
$a + b + c + d = 360°$

<u>Vertically opposite</u> angles are equal.
$a = b, c = d$
$a + c = b + d = 180°$

An <u>exterior angle</u> of a triangle equals the sum of the two opposite <u>interior angles</u>
$a + b = c$

ANGLES AND TESSELLATIONS

EXAMPLES OF ANGLE QUESTIONS

Find the angles labelled by letters:

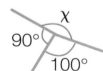

$X + 90^0 + 100^0 = 360^0$
$X = 360^0 - 190^0$
$X = 170^0$.

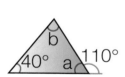

$a + 110^0 = 180^0$
$a = 70^0$.
$70^0 + 40^0 + b = 180^0$
$b = 180^0 - 110^0$
$b = 70^0$.

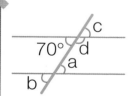

$a = 70^0$ (alternate).
$b = 70^0$ (corresponding).
$c = 70^0$ (corresponding to a).
$d = 180 - 70 = 110^0$
(angles on a straight line).

ANGLES IN POLYGONS

There are two types of angles in a polygon: <u>interior</u> (inside) and <u>exterior</u> (outside).
For a regular polygon with n sides:
- Sum of exterior angles = 360°.
  So exterior angle = $\frac{360°}{n}$
- Interior angle + exterior angle = 180°.
- Sum of interior angles = $(n - 2) \times 180°$.

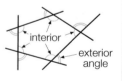

EXAMPLE
Calculate the interior and exterior angle of a regular pentagon.
A pentagon has 5 sides, i.e. n = 5.
Exterior angle = $\frac{360}{5}$ = 72°.
Interior angle + exterior angle = 180°.
Interior angle = 180° − 72°
$\qquad = 108°$.

QUICK TEST

1. Find the size of the angles labelled by letters:

2. Find the size of a) an exterior and

   b) an interior angle of a regular hexagon

a)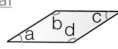

b)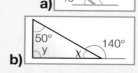

c)

d)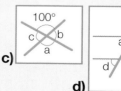

1. a) $a = 140°$ b) $x = 40°$, $y = 90°$ c) $a = 100°$, $b = 80°$, $c = 80°$ d) $a = 50°$, $b = 130°$, $c = 50°$, $d = 50°$ 2. a) $50°$ b) $120°$

COMPASS BEARINGS

The diagram shows the points of the compass.

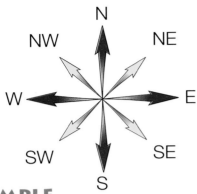

EXAMPLE

If Paulo is facing East and turns clockwise through an angle of 270°, what direction will he now be facing?

> Remember clockwise is this direction.

Paulo will now be facing North.

FIGURE BEARINGS

- Bearings give a direction in degrees.
- Bearings are always measured from the North in a clockwise direction. They must have three figures.

EXAMPLES

Bearing of A from B = 180° – 50° = 130°.

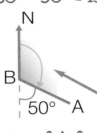

Examiner's Top Tip
The word '_from_' is very important when answering bearings questions. It tells you where to put the North line and measure from.

Bearing of A from B = 360° – 30° = 330°.

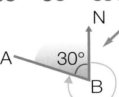

> Measure from the North line at B.

BEARINGS AND SCALE DRAWINGS

SCALE DRAWINGS AND BEARINGS

Scale drawings are very useful for measuring lengths which cannot be measured directly.

EXAMPLE

A ship sails from a harbour for 15 km on a bearing of 040°, and then continues due east for 20 km. Make a scale drawing of this journey using a scale of 1 cm to 5 km. How far will the ship have to sail to get back to the harbour by the shortest route? What will the bearing be?

Shortest route = 6.4 x 5 km = 32 km. Bearing = 70° + 180° = 250°.

SCALE DRAWINGS

Scale drawings are very useful for measuring lengths which cannot be measured directly.

EXAMPLE
Here is a rough sketch of a sector of a circle. Using a scale of 1 cm to 2 m, draw an accurate drawing of the sector.

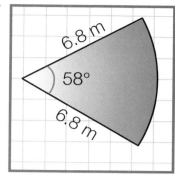

A scale of 1 cm to 2 m means that 6.8 m is $6.8 \div 2 = 3.4$ cm on the diagram.

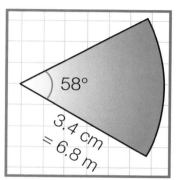

SCALES AND MAPS

Scales are often used on maps. They are usually written as a ratio.

EXAMPLE
The scale on a road map is 1 : 25000. Bury and Oldham are 20 cm apart on the map. Work out the real distance, in km, between Bury and Oldham.

Scale 1 : 25 000, distance on map is 20 cm.
Real distance = 20 x 25 000 = 500 000 cm.
Divide by 100 to change cm to m:
500000 ÷ 100 = 5000 m.
Divide by 1000 to change m to km:
5000 ÷ 1000 = 5 km.

A scale of 1 : 25000 means that 1 cm on the scale drawing represents a real length of 25 000 cm.

BACK BEARINGS

Look for alternate (Z) or corresponding angles.

When finding the <u>back</u> <u>bearing</u> (the bearing of B <u>from</u> A below):
- draw a North line at A
- use the properties of parallel lines, since both North lines are parallel.

EXAMPLES
Bearing of B from A
= 360° – 50°
= 310°.

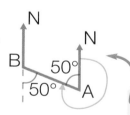

Measure from the North line at A.

Bearing of B from A
= 180° – 30°
= 150°.

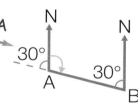

1. What are the bearings of X from Y in the following:

a)

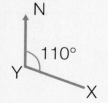

b)

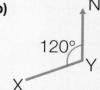

c)

2. For each of the questions above work out the bearings of Y from X.

1. a) 110° b) 240° c) 320° 2. a) 290° b) 060° c) 140°

TRANSLATIONS

These move figures from one place to another. The size and shape of the figure are not changed.
<u>Vectors</u> are used to describe the distance and direction of the translation.
A vector is written as $\begin{bmatrix} a \\ b \end{bmatrix}$. **a** represents the <u>horizontal</u> movement,
and **b** represents the <u>vertical</u> movement.

EXAMPLE
a) Translate ABC by the vector $\begin{bmatrix} 2 \\ 1 \end{bmatrix}$.
   Call it P.

> This means 2 to the right and 1 upwards.

b) Translate ABC by the vector $\begin{bmatrix} -3 \\ -2 \end{bmatrix}$.
   Call it Q.
P and Q are congruent.

> This means 3 to the left and 2 down.

Remember that two shapes are <u>congruent</u>
if one is exactly the same as the other.

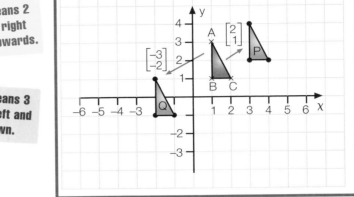

TRANSFORMATIONS

A transformation changes the position or size of a shape.
There are 4 types of transformations: translations,
reflections, rotations and enlargements.

REFLECTIONS

> Count the squares of the object from the mirror.
> It's easier.

These create an image of an object
on the other side of a mirror line.
The mirror line is known as an
axis of reflection. The size and
shape of the figure are not changed.

EXAMPLE
Reflect triangle ABC in:
a)   the x axis, and call it D
b)   the line $y = -x$, and call it E
c)   the line $x = 5$, and call it F.
D, E and F are congruent
to triangle ABC.

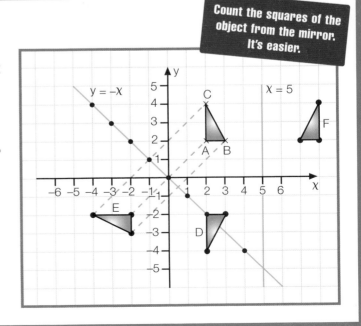

ROTATIONS

These <u>turn</u> a figure through an angle about some fixed point.
This fixed point is called the <u>centre of rotation</u>.
The size and shape of the figure are not changed.

EXAMPLE
Rotate triangle ABC:
(a)   90° clockwise about (0, 0) and call it R
(b)   180° about (0, 0), and call it S
(c)   90° anticlockwise about (−1, 1), and call it T.

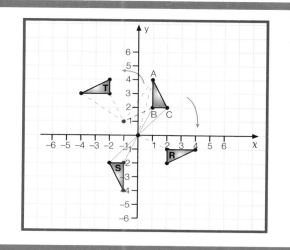

ENLARGEMENTS

- **These change the size but not the shape of an object.**
- **The <u>centre of enlargement</u> is the point from which the enlargement takes place.**
- **The <u>scale factor</u> indicates how many times the length of the original figure has changed size.**
- **If the scale factor is <u>greater than 1</u>, the shape becomes <u>bigger</u>.**
- **If the scale factor is <u>less than 1</u>, the shape becomes <u>smaller</u>.**

Examiner's Top Tip
When describing a rotation give:
- the centre of rotation
- the direction of the turn (clockwise/anticlockwise)
- the angle of the turn.

EXAMPLE
Enlarge shape ABCDEF by a scale factor of 2, centre = (0, 0).
Call it A′ B′ C′ D′ E′ F′

If asked to describe an enlargement, state the centre of enlargement and the scale factor.

Notice that each side of the enlargement is twice the size of the original.
OA′ = 2 x 0A.

EXAMPLE
ABC has been enlarged with a scale factor = $\frac{1}{2}$, to give A′B′C′ the centre of enlargement is at 0.

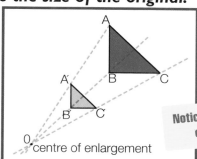

centre of enlargement

Notice that the length of OA′ is $\frac{1}{2}$ OA.

LEVEL 7

- -

QUICK TEST

1. On the diagram on the right:
a)   **Translate ABC by the vector $\begin{bmatrix} -3 \\ 1 \end{bmatrix}$.**
     Call it P
b)   **Reflect ABC in the line y = x.**
     Call it Q
c)   **Reflect ABC in the line y = −1.**
     Call it R
d)   **Rotate ABC 180° about (0, 0).**
     Call it S

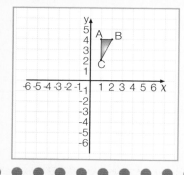

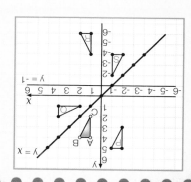

LOCI AND COORDINATES IN 3D

COMMON LOCI

LEVEL 7

Locus must be drawn carefully and measured accurately.

- The locus of a point is the set of all possible positions which that point can occupy, subject to some given condition or rule.
- The plural of locus is <u>loci</u>.

(a) The locus of the points which are a constant distance from a fixed point is a circle.

locus
•P

(b) The locus of the points which are equidistant from two points X and Y is the perpendicular bisector of XY.

perpendicular bisector
X — Y

(c) The locus of the points which are equidistant from two lines is the line which bisects the angle.

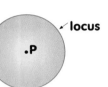
locus

(d) The locus of the points which are a constant distance from a line XY is a pair of parallel lines, above and below XY.

X————————Y

EXAMPLE OF LOCI

LEVEL 7

EXAMPLE
John is redesigning his garden. He wishes to plant a rose tree. The tree must be at least 4 metres from the house, and at least 4 metres from the corner A of the green-house. Show accurately on the diagram the region in which John can plant his rose tree (you would usually be given a scale to use).

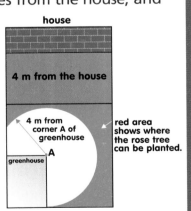

house
4 m from the house
4 m from corner A of greenhouse
red area shows where the rose tree can be planted.
A
greenhouse

COORDINATES IN 3D

LEVEL 7

This involves the extension of the normal x–y coordinates into a third direction, known as z. All positions then have three coordinates (x, y, z).

EXAMPLE
For the cuboid the vertices would have the following coordinates:
A (3, 0, 0)
B (3, 2, 0)
C (0, 2, 0)
D (0, 2, 1)
E (0, 0, 1)
F (3, 0, 1)
G (3, 2, 1)
0 (0, 0, 0)

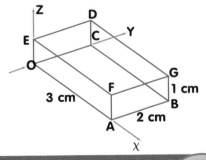

3 cm
2 cm
1 cm

QUICK TEST

LEVEL 7

1. A gold coin is buried in the rectangular field. It is:
- **4 metres from T**
- **equidistant from RU and RS**

Mark with an X the position of the gold coin.

(Note: draw the diagram with a scale of 1 cm to 1 m to answer this properly.)

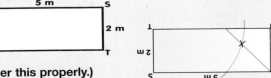

R — 5 m — S
2 m
U — T

PYTHAGORAS' THEOREM

DEFINITION OF PYTHAGORAS' THEOREM

LEVEL 7

The <u>hypotenuse</u> is the longest side of a right-angled triangle. It is always opposite the right angle.

Pythagoras' Theorem states: in any right-angled triangle, the square on the hypotenuse is equal to the sum of the squares on the other two sides.

Pythagoras' Theorem allows you to calculate the length of a side, providing the lengths of the other two sides in a right angled triangle are known.

Using the letters in the diagram the theorem is written as:
$c^2 = a^2 + b^2$

This may be rearranged to give:
$b^2 = c^2 - a^2$
$a^2 = c^2 - b^2$

These are useful when calculating shorter sides.

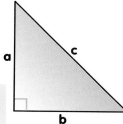

FINDING A MISSING LENGTH

Rearrange the formula and use $a^2 = c^2 - b^2$.

EXAMPLE
Find the length of XY, giving your answer to 1 d.p. Using Pythagoras' Theorem gives:

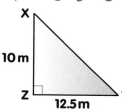

$XY^2 = XZ^2 + ZY^2$
$= 10^2 + 12.5^2$
$XY^2 = 256.25$
$XY = \sqrt{256.25}$
(square root to find XY)
$= 16.0$ m (1 d.p.)

EXAMPLE
Find the length of CD, giving your answer to 1 d.p. Using Pythagoras' Theorem gives:

$CE^2 = CD^2 + DE^2$
$CD^2 = CE^2 - DE^2$
$CD^2 = 12^2 - 4.2^2$
$CD^2 = 126.36$
$CD = \sqrt{126.36}$
11.2 m (1 d.p.)

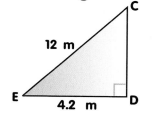

CALCULATING THE LENGTH OF A LINE AB, GIVEN TWO SETS OF COORDINATES

LEVEL 7

By drawing in a triangle between the two points A (1, 2) and B (7, 6) we can find the length of AB by Pythagoras' Theorem.
Horizontal distance = 6 (7 − 1)
Vertical distance = 4 (6 − 2)
Length of $(AB)^2 = 6^2 + 4^2$
$(AB)^2 = 36 + 16$
$(AB)^2 = 52$
$(AB)^2 = \sqrt{52}$
Length of AB = 7.21

The <u>midpoint</u> of AB, M has coordinates (4, 4) i.e. $\dfrac{(1 + 7)}{2}, \dfrac{(2 + 6)}{2}$

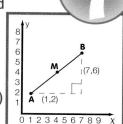

Problems
Pythagoras' Theorem can be used to solve practical problems.

EXAMPLE
Seagull Point is 12.5 km West and 6.7 km North of Fisherman's Cove. Calculate the direct distance from Seagull Point to Fisherman's Cove. Call the distance between Seagull Point and Fisherman's Cove X.

$X^2 = 12.5^2 + 6.7^2$
$X^2 = 201.14$
$X = \sqrt{201.14}$
$X = 14.2$ km (1 d.p.)

QUICK TEST

C) 1. Calculate the lengths of the sides marked with a letter. Give your answer to 1 d.p.

a) 12m, x, 6.9 m

b) 15.2m, 7.3 m, y

C) 2. A ship sets off from Port A and travels 50 km North then 80 km East to reach Port B. How far is Port A from Port B, by the shortest route?

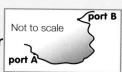
Not to scale — port B — port A

1.a) 13.8 m b) 13.3 m 2. 94.3 km

METRIC UNITS

Length	Weight	Capacity
10 mm = 1 cm	1000 mg = 1 g	1000 ml = 1 litre
100 cm = 1 m	1000 g = 1 kg	100 cl = 1 litre
1000 m = 1 km	1000 kg = 1 tonne	1000 cm³ = 1 litre

Try and remember these metric equivalents.

CONVERTING UNITS

- If changing from small units to large units (e.g. g to kg) divide.
- If changing from large units to small units (e.g. km to metres) multiply.

EXAMPLES

500 cm = 5 metres (÷ 100)
5 litres = 500 cl (x 100)
3500 g = 3.5 kg (÷ 1000)
25 cm = 250 mm (x 10)

THE CALENDAR

A year has 12 months:

JUNE
S M T W T F S
1 2 3 4 5 6
7 8 9 10 11 12 13
14 15 16 17 18 19 20
21 22 23 24 25 26 27
28 29 30

January	31 days
February	28 or 29 days
March	31 days
April	30 days
May	31 days
June	30 days
July	31 days
August	31 days
September	30 days
October	31 days
November	30 days
December	31 days

There are 365 days in a year. In a leap year there are 366 days because February has 29 days in a leap year.

MEASURES AND MEASUREMENT ①

IMPERIAL UNITS

Length	Weight	Capacity
1 foot = 12 inches	1 stone = 14 pounds (lb)	20 fluid oz = 1 pint
1 yard = 3 feet	1 pound = 16 ounces (oz)	8 pints = 1 gallon

COMPARISONS BETWEEN METRIC AND IMPERIAL UNITS

Length	Weight	Capacity
2.5 cm ≈ 1 inch	25 g ≈ 1 ounce	1 litre ≈ $1\frac{3}{4}$ pints
30 cm ≈ 1 foot	1 kg ≈ 2.2 pounds	4.5 litres ≈ 1 gallon
1 metre ≈ 39 inches		
8 km ≈ 5 miles		

You should know these approximate conversions. Ask somebody to test you.

EXAMPLE

Change 8 inches into cm.
1 inch ≈ 2.5 cm
8 inches ≈ 8 x 2.5 = 20 cm

Check to see if your answer sounds sensible.

READING SCALES

Decimals are usually used when reading off scales. Measuring jugs, rulers and weighing scales are all examples of scales which have decimals.

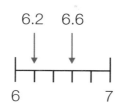

EXAMPLES

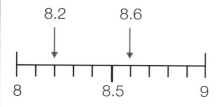

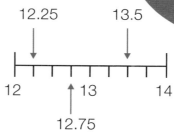

There are 10 spaces between the 8 and the 9. Each space is 0.1.

There are five spaces between the 6 and the 7. Each space is 0.2.

There are four spaces between the 12 and 13. Each space is 0.25.

ACCURACY OF MEASUREMENT

LEVEL 7

CONTINUOUS MEASUREMENTS
- These are measurements which have been made by using a measuring instrument; for example the height of a person.
- Continuous measures are not exact.

EXAMPLE

Lucy is 167 cm tall correct to the nearest cm. Her actual height could be anywhere between 166.5 cm and 167.5 cm.

−0.5   +0.5

166 cm   166.5   167 cm   167.5   168 cm

Remember that these measurements cannot be equal to the upper limit.

These two values are the limits of Lucy's height. If H represents height, then
$166.5 \leq H < 167.5$

In general, if a measurement is accurate to some given amount, then the true value lies within a maximum of a half a unit of that amount.

This is the <u>lower limit</u> of Lucy's height. Anything below 167.5 is recorded as 167 cm.

This is the <u>upper limit</u> of Lucy's height. Anything from 166.5 upwards would be recorded as 167 cm.

QUICK TEST

LEVEL 7

1. Change 6 200 g into kg.
2. Change 4.2 cm into mm.
3. Change 6 litres into pints.
4. What do the pointers on the scales represent?
5. Write down the upper and lower limits for a time of 6.3 seconds, rounded to the nearest tenth of a second.

A   B   C   E   G
9   10   2.4   2.5   6   7
                              D   F

1. 6.2 kg   2. 42 mm   3. 10.5 pints   4. A = 9.2   B = 9.5   C = 2.42   D = 2.46   E = 2.48   F = 6.25   G = 6.75   5. 6.25 ≤ 6.3 < 6.35

COMPOUND MEASURES

Speed can be measured in kilometres per hour (km/h), miles per hour (m.p.h.) and metres per second (m/s). Km/h, m.p.h. and m/s are all <u>compound</u> <u>measures</u>, because they involve a combination of basic measures – in this case distance and time.

> Just remember the letters
> – it is quicker.

SPEED

| Average speed = $\dfrac{\text{total distance travelled}}{\text{total time taken}} = \dfrac{D}{T}$ |

From the speed formula two other formulae can be found.

| Time = $\dfrac{\text{distance}}{\text{speed}}$ | distance = speed x time |

Always check the units first, before starting a question and change them if necessary.

Use this triangle to help you remember the formulae.

EXAMPLE
Lynette walks 10 km in 4 hours.
Find her average speed.
$S = \dfrac{D}{T} = \dfrac{10}{4} = 2.5$ km/h

EXAMPLE
Mr Singh drove a distance of 500 miles at an average speed of 70 m.p.h. How long did the journey take?
$T = \dfrac{D}{S} = \dfrac{500}{70} = 7.14\ldots$ hours

> This answer does not mean 7 hours 14 minutes.

7.14... hours must be changed into hours and minutes.
· Subtract the hours 7.14... – 7 = 0.14... hours.
· Multiply the decimal part by 60 minutes.
    0.14... x 60 = 8.6 = 9 minutes to the nearest minute.
Time = 7 hours 9 minutes.

> Use this triangle to help you remember the formulae.

DENSITY

| Density = $\dfrac{\text{mass}}{\text{volume}}$ $D = \dfrac{M}{V}$ | Volume = $\dfrac{\text{mass}}{\text{density}}$ $V = \dfrac{M}{D}$ | Mass = density x volume $M = D \times V$ |

> Since the mass is in grams and the volume in cm³, density is in g/cm³.

EXAMPLE
Find the density of an object whose mass is 600 g and whose volume is 50 cm³. Density = $\dfrac{M}{V} = \dfrac{600}{50} = 12$ g/cm³.

12- AND 24-HOUR CLOCK TIMES

> **Examiner's Top Tip**
> The formula triangles for speed and density are very useful when working out which formula to use. Working out the units of speed and density also needs care.

The 12-hour clock uses <u>a.m.</u> and <u>p.m.</u>
a.m. means before <u>midday</u>, p.m. means after <u>midday</u>.

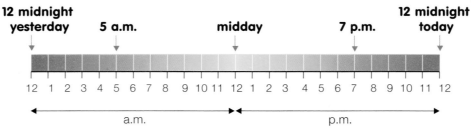

> Remember to write in 'a.m.' and 'p.m.' for 12-hour clock times.

The <u>24-hour</u> <u>clock</u> numbers the hours from 0 to 23.
It is written using four figures.

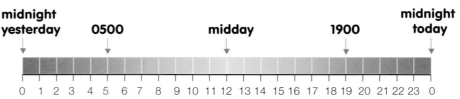

You need to be able to write times using both the 12-hour and 24-hour clock.

EXAMPLES
2:42 p.m. is the same as 1442   1534 is the same as 3:34 p.m.
4:30 a.m. is the same as 0430   0904 is the same as 9:04 a.m.

MEASURES AND MEASUREMENT ②

TIMETABLES

> There will be a train from London every 60 minutes, i.e. 0750, 0850.

Timetables often use 24-hour clock time. Timetables should be read carefully.

EXAMPLE

The train timetable illustrates the train times from London to Manchester.

London, Euston	0602	0650	Every 60	1100	1300
Watford Junction	0632	0720	minutes	1130	1330
Stoke-on-Trent	0750	0838	until	-	1445
Manchester, Piccadilly	0838	0926		1315	1540

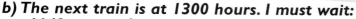

The 0750 train from Stoke-on-Trent

The 0650 train from London arrives in Manchester at 0926.

The 1100 from London does not stop at Stoke-on-Trent.

> If the timetable is written in 24-hour clock times, make sure your answers are in 24-hour clock times.

a) Diana is travelling from Watford Junction to Manchester, Piccadilly. If she catches the 0602 train, how long is her journey?

b) If I arrive at London, Euston at 1142, how long do I have to wait for the next train to Manchester?

a) 0632   0838   Time = 2 hours 6 minutes
   Depart   Arrive
   Watford Junction   Manchester

> Remember there are only 60 minutes in 1 hour.

b) The next train is at 1300 hours. I must wait:
   1142   →   1200 = 18 minutes   I wait one hour 18 minutes
   1200   →   1300 = one hour

TIME FACTS

There are 60 seconds in one minute.
There are 60 minutes in one hour.
There are 24 hours in one day.
There are seven days in one week.
There are 52 weeks in one year.

This clock has two hands.
The short hand tells us the hour,
and the long hand tells us the minutes.
For the hour hand each mark is one hour.
For the minute hand each mark is five minutes.

This clock reads 10 past 7.

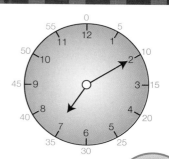

LEVEL 7

QUICK TEST

1. It takes Bina 30 minutes to walk to the shop 2 km away. At what speed is she travelling?

2. The mass of an object is 500 grams. If the density is 6.2 g/cm³ what is the volume of the object?

3. Bonnie travels to work at a speed of 40 m.p.h. If she works 30 miles away, how long will it take her to get to work?

4. Write these times using the 24 hour clock: a) 6:32 pm b) 8:27 am c) 2:34 am d) 9:36 pm

1. 4 km/h 2. 80.65 3. 45 minutes 4. a) 1832 b) 0827 c) 0234 d) 2136

ESTIMATING THE AREA AND FINDING THE PERIMETER OF 2D SHAPES

EXAMPLE
Find the perimeter of this shape:
Perimeter = 4 + 5 + 3 + 2.7 + 2.7
= 17.4 cm

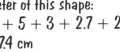
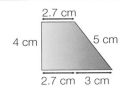
2.7 cm
4 cm   5 cm
2.7 cm   3 cm

Areas of irregular shapes can be estimated by counting the squares the shape covers.

EXAMPLE
· Label the squares as you count them.
· Try to match up parts of squares to make a whole one.

| The shape has an area of 20.5 units². | → | It is cm² when each square is 1 cm². |

1	2	3	4
5	6	7	8
9	10	11	12
13	14	15	16
17	18	19	

these make 1 whole square

this is ½ a square

AREA AND PERIMETER OF 2D SHAPES

Perimeter – this is the distance around the outside edge of a shape.
Area – this is the amount of space a 2D shape covers. Common units of area are mm², cm², m², etc.

AREAS OF QUADRILATERALS AND TRIANGLES

AREA OF A RECTANGLE
Area = length x width
A = l x w

Width
Length

Write the formulae using letters – it's quicker. Area = length x width A = l x w.

AREA OF A PARALLELOGRAM
Area = base x perpendicular height
A = b x h

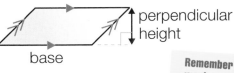
perpendicular height
base

Remember to work out the brackets first.

AREA OF A TRIANGLE
A = ½ x base x perpendicular height
A = ½ x b x h

perpendicular height
base

Remember perpendicular height just means the height which is 90° to the base.

AREA OF A TRAPEZIUM
A = ½ x (sum of parallel sides)
x perpendicular height between sides
A = ½ x (a + b) x h

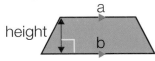
a
height
b

EXAMPLES - Find the area of the following shapes.
A = ½ x b x h
A = ½ x 7 x 5 = 17.5 cm²

5 cm
7 cm

A = ½ x (a + b) x h
A = ½ x (10 + 8) x 5
= 45 cm²

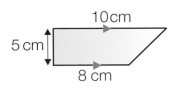
10 cm
5 cm
8 cm

CIRCUMFERENCE AND AREA OF A CIRCLE

Circumference = π × diameter $C = π × d$
= 2 × π × radius = 2 × π × r
Area = π × (radius)² $A = π × r^2$

radius
diameter
circumference

EXAMPLE
Find the circumference and area of this circle:
Use π = 3.14

10 cm

$C = π × d$
= 3.14 × 10
= 31.4 cm
$A = π × r^2$ (r = 10 ÷ 2 = 5)
A = 3.14 × 5²
= 78.5 cm²

Remember r² means r × r.

Remember that the circumference of a circle is the distance around the outside edge.

EXAMPLE
Mohammed's bicycle wheel has a diameter of 60 cm. Work out the circumference of the wheel, using π = 3.14.

Use π = 3.14 or the value of π on your calculator, if you are not told its value in the question.

$C = π × d$
C = 3.14 × 60
C = 188.4 cm
If Mohammed travels a distance of 50 metres on the bicycle, how many times does his wheel turn around?
Change 50 m into cm first, i.e. 50 × 100 = 5000 cm
Distance ÷ circumference = no. of turns.
$\frac{5000}{188.4}$ = 26.5 times

Always check the units are the same before starting a question.

The wheel must turn 27 times to go a distance of 50 metres.

Check that the answer is sensible.

EXAMPLE
Find the area of a circular rose garden, which has a diameter of 2.6 metres. Use π = 3.142.
Diameter = 2.6 m Radius = 2.6 ÷ 2 = 1.3 m
Area = π × r²
= 3.142 × 1.3² Remember 1.3² means 1.3 × 1.3
= 5.3 m² (1 d.p.)

LEVEL 7

AREAS OF ENLARGEMENTS AND CHANGING AREA UNITS

This usually catches everybody out. If a shape is enlarged by a scale factor n then:
The <u>AREAS</u> are n² times bigger.

EXAMPLE
If n = 2:
• the <u>lengths</u> are twice as big
• the area is 4 times as big (n² = 4).

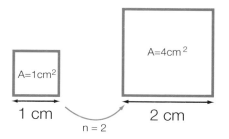

A=1cm²
1 cm
n = 2
A=4cm²
2 cm

EXAMPLE
The square has a length of 1 metre.

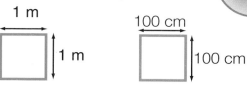

1 m
1 m

100 cm
100 cm

This is the same as a length of 100 cm.
Area = 1 m²   Area = 10000 cm²
Therefore 1 m² = 10000 cm²
(not 100 as most people think!)
Because of this possible mistake it's always better to change the units before you start a question.

LEVEL 7

QUICK TEST

C 1. Work out the area of the following shapes, giving your answer to 1 d.p.

C 2. Work out the circumference of a circle with a radius of 4.9 cm. Use π = 3.14.

3. Change 40 000 cm² into m².

4. The area of a shape is 3 cm². If the lengths are enlarged by a scale factor of 3 what is the area of the enlarged shape?

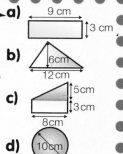

a)
9 cm
3 cm

b)
6cm
12 cm

c)
5cm
3cm
8cm

d)
10cm

1. a) 27 cm² b) 36 cm² c) 44 cm² d) 78.5 cm² 2. 30.8 cm (1 d.p.) 3. 4 m² 4. 27 cm²

ESTIMATING AND CALCULATING VOLUMES OF 3D SHAPES

VOLUME – this is the amount of space a 3D shape occupies.

Common units of volume are mm^3, cm^3, m^3, etc.

The volume of a 3D shape can be found by counting the number of $1 cm^3$ cubes.

EXAMPLE

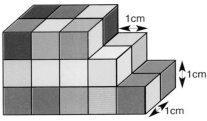

The volume of this shape is $24 cm^3$.
This cube has a volume of $1 cm^3$ (1 cubic centimetre).

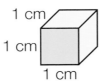

VOLUME OF A CUBOID

Volume =
length x width x height
$V = l \times w \times h$

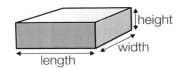

VOLUME OF A PRISM

Volume =
area of cross-section x length
$V = a \times l$

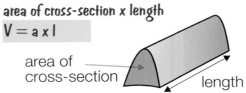

area of cross-section

length

A prism is any solid which can be cut into slices, which are all the same shape. This is called having a <u>uniform cross-section</u>.

VOLUME OF A CYLINDER

Volume = area of cross-section x length

$$V = \pi r^2 \times h$$

Area of circle   Height or length

radius

height

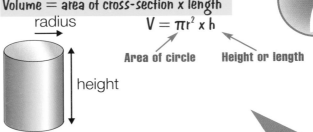

EXAMPLE

Dog food is sold in a cylindrical tin.
Work out the volume of dog food the tin contains.
Use $\pi = 3.14$
Diameter = $8 cm$
i.e. Radius = $4 cm$
$V = \pi \times r^2 \times h$
$V = 3.14 \times 4^2 \times 10$
$V = 502.4 cm^3$

8 cm
DOGGO'S
10 cm

EXAMPLE

A door wedge is in the shape of a trapezium.
Work out the volume of the door wedge.

Substitute values in carefully and show full working out.

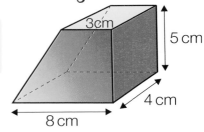

3 cm
5 cm
4 cm
8 cm

Area of cross-section:
$$A = \frac{(a + b) \times h}{2}$$
$$A = \frac{(3 + 8) \times 5}{2} = 27.5 cm^2$$

Volume = $27.5 \times 4 = 110 cm^3$

Remember, to find the volume, multiply the area of cross-section by the length.

VOLUMES OF ENLARGEMENTS

Just like other areas these usually catch people out!
For an enlargement of <u>scale factor n</u>:
The volumes are <u>n^3</u> times bigger.

EXAMPLE

If a cube of length 1 cm is enlarged
by a scale factor of 2:
i.e. n = 2 so $V = 2^3$ = 8 times bigger

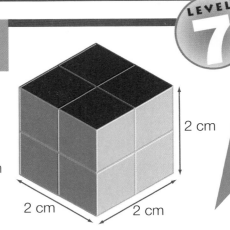

2 cm

1 cm

1 cm   1 cm

2 cm   2 cm

volume = 1 cm³   **volume = 8 cm³**

CONVERTING VOLUME UNITS

Another tricky topic which usually catches everybody out!

EXAMPLE

The cube has a length of 1 m –
this is the same as a length of 100 cm.

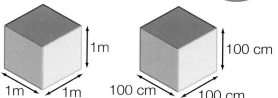

volume = 1 m³   volume = 1 000 000 cm³

Therefore 1 m³ = 1 000 000 cm³   not quite what you may think!

It's probably better therefore to change all the lengths to the same unit before starting a question!

VOLUME OF 3D SHAPES

QUICK TEST

c

1. Work out the volume of these 3D shapes, giving your answer to 1 d.p.

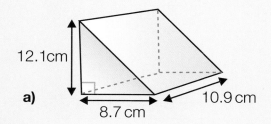

a)
12.1cm
8.7 cm
10.9 cm

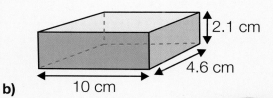

b)
2.1 cm
4.6 cm
10 cm

LEVEL 7

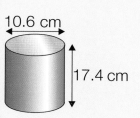

10.6 cm
17.4 cm
c)

2. A cuboid has a volume of 6 cm³.

If the cuboid is enlarged by a scale factor of 2, calculate the volume of the enlarged solid

LEVEL 7

Examiner's Top Tip

- Change all the lengths to the same units before starting!
- Remember to put in your units at the end.
- You will need to learn the formulae for the cuboid and cylinder.

SHAPE, SPACE AND MEASURES

1. From the box below, choose the correct unit to complete the statements:

| cm | kg | km | g | ml | l | m | mm |

a) The width of a book is about 17 ....
b) Fiona's mother weighed 52 ....
c) A giraffe is about 5.......tall
d) A mug holds about 250.......of water
e) The height of the classroom would be about 3.........

2. Write down what each of these pointers show: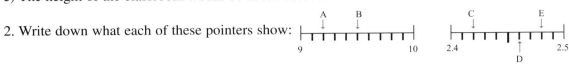

3. a) On the rectangle draw on the lines of symmetry
   b) What is the order of rotational symmetry of the rectangle?

4. Write down the order
of rotational symmetry, if any,
of these shapes:

5. 72° 241° 379° 127° 83° 90° 41°
Which of these angles are:
a) acute .... b) obtuse .... c) reflex .... d) right-angled ....

6. Find the size of the angles marked with a letter:

7. Each cube has a volume of 1 cm^3.
Calculate the volume of this shape

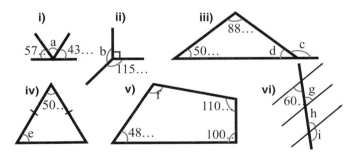

8. a) Change 6200 g into kg ....
   b) Change 4.2 cm into mm ....
   c) Change 6 litres into pints ....

9. Draw:
a) the plan of the solid
b) the elevations of the solid as seen from A and B

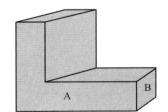

10. Work out the area of the following shapes, giving your answer to 1 d.p.

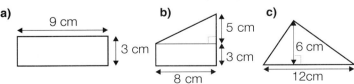

a) 9 cm 3 cm
b) 5 cm 3 cm 8 cm
c) 6 cm 12cm

11. Work out the area of the following shapes, giving your answers to 3 s.f.

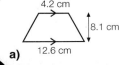 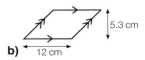   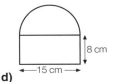

a) 4.2 cm 8.1 cm 12.6 cm
b) 5.3 cm 12 cm
c) 9 cm
d) 8 cm 15 cm

c 12. Work out the circumference of a circle with a radius of 4.9 cm.
Use π = 3.14

c 13. Calculate the area of the shaded region. Use π = 3.14

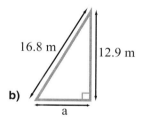

14. What are the bearings of X from Y in the following:

a)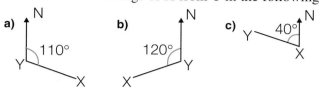

N
110°
Y
X

b)
N
120°
X
Y

c)
Y 40°
N
X

15. a) Reflect shape A in the x axis. Call it B
b) Rotate shape A 90° anticlockwise about (0, 0). Call it C
c) Translate shape A by $\binom{-4}{-6}$. Call it D
d) Enlarge shape A by a scale factor of 2.
Centre of enlargement at (0, 0). Call it E

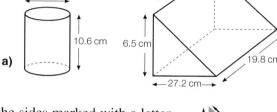

c 16. Work out the volume of the
following 3D shapes.
Give your answer to 3 s.f.

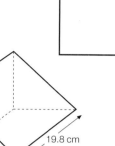

85 mm
10.6 cm
a)

b)
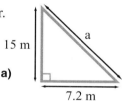
6.5 cm
19.8 cm
27.2 cm

c 17. Calculate the lengths of the sides marked with a letter.
Give your answer to 1 d.p.

7 18. Calculate the area of this triangle:

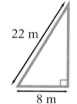
22 m
8 m

a)
15 m
a
7.2 m

b)
16.8 m
12.9 m
a

7 19. Change 7 m² into cm². ....

7 20. If the volume of a cuboid is 7 m³, work out the volume of the cuboid if the lengths are enlarged by a scale factor of 2.

....

7 21. Write down the upper and lower limits for a time of 9.2 seconds,
rounded to the nearest tenth of a second.

....

7 22. Write down the 3D coordinates for each letter on the solid.

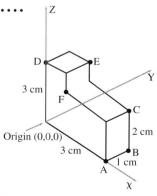

Z
D E
3 cm
F
Y
Origin (0,0,0)
3 cm
C
2 cm
B
A 1 cm
X

How did you do?

1 – 5	correct	....start again
5–11	correct	....getting there
12–17	correct	....good work
18–22	correct	....excellent

TYPES OF DATA

- <u>Discrete data</u> – each category is separate. It is often found by counting. Examples include the number of red cars in a car park.
- <u>Continuous data</u> – here the values change from one category to the next. Such data is often found by measuring. Examples include the height and shoe size of year 8 pupils.
- <u>Primary data</u> – data that you collect yourself.
- <u>Secondary data</u> – data that somebody else has collected (e.g. census).

STEM AND LEAF DIAGRAMS

Stem and leaf diagrams are another way of recording information.

EXAMPLE
The heights in cm of some students are:
154, 172, 160, 164, 168, 177, 181, 140, 142, 153, 154, 153, 162
Putting this information into a stem and leaf diagram would look like this:

14	0	2		
15	4	3	4	3
16	0	4	8	2
17	2	7		
18	1			

stem = 10 cm

For the value 142 cm the stem is 14 and the leaf is 2.

This shows that to read off the values you have to multiply the stem by 10 and add on the leaf.

In a stem and leaf diagram, all the individual values are recorded. You can read them off the diagram. To organise the data more, the leaves should be written in order.

14	0	2		
15	3	3	4	4
16	0	2	4	8
17	2	7		
18	1			

SURVEYS AND QUESTIONNAIRES

- Data can be collected by carrying out <u>surveys</u> using <u>questionnaires</u>.
- A <u>hypothesis</u> is a prediction which can be tested and usually gives a purpose to the survey. e.g. most staff at the school have a red car.
- An <u>observation</u> <u>sheet</u> is used to collect data. It must be clear and easy to use.

Examiner's Top Tip
When asked to write a questionnaire always word your questions very carefully. Tick boxes are useful when sorting your information.

LEVEL 7

EXAMPLE

Colour of staff cars

Colour	Tally	Frequency
red		
blue		
white		
green		
black		
others		

QUESTIONNAIRES
When designing questionnaires:
- Keep the questionnaire short.
- Give instructions on how to fill it in.
- Ask questions which cover the purpose of your survey.
- Do not ask for information which is not needed, e.g. name.
- Make sure that your opinion is not evident, e.g. do you agree that <u>Neighbours</u> is better than <u>Home and Away</u>?
- Allow for any possible outcomes.

EXAMPLE
How much do you spend on magazines each week?

Under £1 ☐ £1 – £1.99 ☐ £2 – £2.99 ☐ £3 or over ☐

Word any questions you write very carefully.

COLLECTING DATA

COLLECTING INFORMATION

- Data which has been collected can be sorted by putting it into a table called a <u>tally chart</u> or <u>frequency</u> <u>table</u>.
- The tally chart shows the frequency of each item (how often the item occurs).
- A tally is just a line I, which when grouped into fives make them easier to count. The fifth one forms a gate, i.e. ⊮.

GROUPING DATA

If the data covers a large range of results, it is usual to group the data into <u>class intervals</u>, where each class interval is the same width. For continuous data the class <u>intervals</u> are often written using inequalities.

EXAMPLE

To help: cross off the data as you put it in the table.

The heights in cm of 30 pupils were:

137	142	139	120	152
126	149	147	138	135
135	132	127	154	150
138	144	149	150	122
140	142	138	141	149
127	125	141	140	135

- The data has been grouped into class intervals of 5.
- Choose sensible groupings of 2, 5 or 10.
- Check that all data has been included.

Height (cm)	Tally	Frequency
$120 \leq h < 125$	II	2
$125 \leq h < 130$	IIII	4
$130 \leq h < 135$	I	1
$135 \leq h < 140$	⊮ III	8
$140 \leq h < 145$	⊮ II	7
$145 \leq h < 150$	IIII	4
$150 \leq h < 155$	IIII	4
	Total	30

Always check the total at the end to make sure all data is included.

$120 \leq h < 125$ means that the heights are all between 120 and 125 cm.

$120 \leq h$ means that the height can be equal to 120 cm.

$h < 125$ means that the height cannot be equal to 125 cm. It would be in the next group.

QUICK TEST

1. Richard and Tammy are carrying out a survey on some students' favourite foods. Design a data collection sheet that they could use.
2. Draw a stem and leaf diagram for this data:
   206, 241, 243, 237, 239, 231, 246, 222, 215, 214, 209, 213, 227
   use stem = 10

1.
| Food type | Tally | Frequency |

2.
20	6	9		
21	3	4	5	
22	2	7		
23	1	9		
24	1	3	6	

24	1	3	6
23	7	1	9
22	7	2	
21	4	3	5
20	9	6	
Frequency	Tally	Food type	

REPRESENTING INFORMATION

BAR CHARTS AND PICTOGRAMS

Data can be shown in several ways using different types of diagrams.

BAR CHARTS
A bar chart is a set of bars or columns of equal width. They show the important features of a set of results. The height of each bar is used to show the frequency. There should be gaps between the bars. The gaps should be as narrow as possible.

PICTOGRAMS
Pictograms use symbols where each symbol represents a certain number of items.

Bar line graphs are similar to bar charts except only a line is drawn.

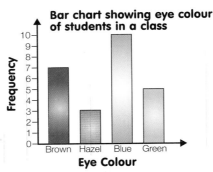

PIE CHARTS

Multiply by 360°

These are circles split up into sections. Each section represents a certain number of items.

CALCULATING ANGLES FOR A PIE CHART
* Find the total for the items listed.
* Find the fraction of the total for each item.
* Multiply the fraction by 360° to find the angle.

Remember there are 360° at the centre of the circle.

EXAMPLE
The favourite sports of 24 students in year 9 are as follows:

Sport	Frequency
Football	9
Swimming	5
Netball	3
Hockey	7

FINDING THE ANGLE
9 out of 24 like football,
i.e. $\frac{9}{24} \times 360° = 135°$
Key in on the calculator:
9 ÷ 24 × 360 =

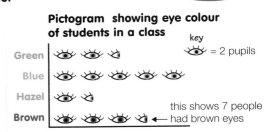
A pie chart showing favourite sport

Football $= \frac{9}{24} \times 360° = 135°$
Swimming $= \frac{5}{24} \times 360° = 75°$
Netball $= \frac{3}{24} \times 360° = 45°$
Hockey $= \frac{7}{24} \times 360° = \underline{105°}$
Total $= 360°$

Check that your angles add up to 360°.

INTERPRETING PIE CHARTS
The pie chart shows how some students travel to school. There are 18 students in total.
How many travel by:
a) Car? b) Bus? c) Walking?
360° = 18 students
$1° = \frac{18}{360°} = 0.05$ (work out 1°)

Car = 60° × 0.05 = 3 students
Bus = 80° × 0.05 = 4 students
Walk = 220° × 0.05 = 11 students

Measure the angles carefully with a protractor.

FREQUENCY DIAGRAMS

- These are drawn to illustrate <u>continuous</u> data.
- They are similar to bar charts except there are no gaps between the bars.
- The data must be grouped into equal class intervals if the length of the bar is used to represent the frequency.

EXAMPLE

The heights of 30 pupils are grouped as shown in the table.

Height (cm)	Frequency
$120 \le h < 125$	2
$125 \le h < 130$	4
$130 \le h < 135$	1
$135 \le h < 140$	8
$140 \le h < 145$	7
$145 \le h < 150$	4
$150 \le h < 155$	4
	30

- The axes do not need to start at zero.
- Do not leave a gap between the bars.
- Label the axes and write a title.

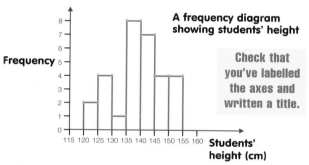

A frequency diagram showing students' height

> Check that you've labelled the axes and written a title.

FREQUENCY POLYGONS

- These are used to join the midpoints of the class intervals for grouped or continuous data.
- To draw the frequency polygon, put a cross on the middle of the bar and join the crosses up with a ruler.
- Draw a line down from the middle of the first and last bar to the x axis.

EXAMPLE

Consider the frequency diagram of the students' height.

LEVEL **7**

> A frequency polygon is said to show the <u>trend</u> of the data.

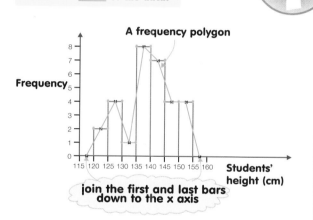

A frequency polygon

join the first and last bars down to the x axis

LINE GRAPHS

These are a set of points joined by a line. Line graphs can be used to show continuous data.

EXAMPLE

Year	1989	1990	1991	1992	1993	1994	1995	1996
Number of cars sold	420	530	480	560	590	620	490	440

The <u>middle values</u> (for example point Y) have no meaning. Point Y does not mean that halfway between 1994 and 1995, 550 cars were sold.

> This can also be referred to as a time series since time is represented on the horizontal axis.

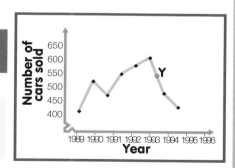

QUICK TEST

1. A chocolate firm asked 1440 students which type of chocolate they preferred. The pie chart shows the results. How many people preferred:

   a) White chocolate? b) Fruit and nut? c) Milk chocolate?

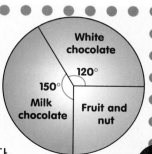

1. a) 480 b) 360 c) 600

DRAWING SCATTER DIAGRAMS

Examiner's Top Tip
Do not rush when drawing a scatter diagram. Plot the points very carefully. In the KS3 SATS you must be able to describe the types of correlation.

• *Work out the scales first before starting. Plot the points carefully, ticking off each point in the table as it is plotted.*

EXAMPLE
The data shows the age of several cars and how much they are now worth.

Age (years)	1	8	4	7	6	3	5	7	3	5	2
Price (£)	5200	1200	3400	1800	2800	4000	1800	2400	4400	3000	5000

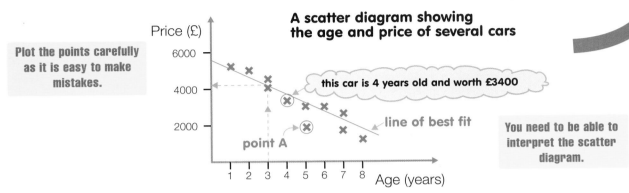

Plot the points carefully as it is easy to make mistakes.

A scatter diagram showing the age and price of several cars

this car is 4 years old and worth £3400

line of best fit

point A

You need to be able to interpret the scatter diagram.

Price (£) — 6000, 4000, 2000 vs *Age (years)* — 1 2 3 4 5 6 7 8

• **The scatter diagram shows that the older the cars become the less they are worth, i.e. there is a <u>negative</u> <u>correlation</u>.**

• **<u>Point A</u> shows a car which is five years old and worth £1800. This is slightly less than expected and may be due to rust or a dent, or the make, etc.**

MISLEADING GRAPHS

Statistical graphs are sometimes misleading; they do not tell the true story.

EXAMPLES
This graph is misleading because it has no scales and the bars are not the same width.

This graph is misleading because the scales do not start at zero, so the growth looks much bigger than it actually is.

This pictogram is misleading because the pictures change size. Although Brand B has only sold twice the amount of Brand A it gives the impression of having sold much more.

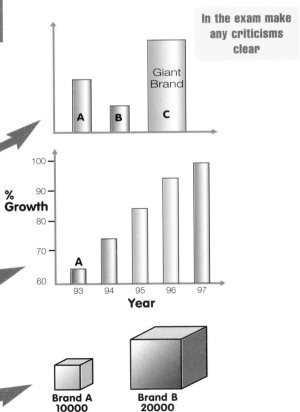

In the exam make any criticisms clear

Giant Brand

A   B   C

% Growth — 100, 90, 80, 70, 60

A

93   94   95   96   97

Year

Brand A
10000
sold

Brand B
20000
sold

LINE OF BEST FIT

- This is the line which 'best fits' the data. It goes in the direction of the data and has roughly the same number of points above the line as below it.
- A line of 'best fit' can be used to make predictions.

LEVEL 7

EXAMPLE

Sandra wishes to sell her car. If it is 3 years old roughly how much would she expect to receive?

- Go across to 3 years on the horizontal axis on the diagram [opposite]. Read up to the line of best fit and then read across. Approximately £4100.

SCATTER DIAGRAMS AND MISLEADING GRAPHS

- A scatter diagram (scattergraph) is used to show two sets of data at the same time.
- It is used to show the connection (correlation) between two sets of data.

TYPES OF CORRELATION

There are three types of correlation: <u>positive</u>, <u>negative</u> or <u>zero</u>.

POSITIVE CORRELATION

This is when as one value increases so does the other. If the points are nearly on a straight line it is said to have a <u>high</u> <u>positive</u> <u>correlation</u>.

NEGATIVE CORRELATION

This is when as one value increases the other decreases. If the points are nearly on a straight line it is said to have a <u>high</u> <u>negative</u> correlation.

ZERO CORRELATION

This is when there is no connection between the values.

QUICK TEST

1. Look at the 2 graphs. a) What does Graph 1 tell you about the relationship between the number of ice lollies sold and the temperature?
b) What does Graph 2 tell you about the relationship between the number of cups of tea sold and the temperature?

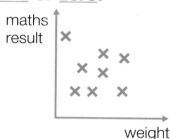

1. a) As the temperature increases, more ice lollies are sold (positive correlation)   b) As the temperature increases, fewer cups of tea are sold (negative correlation)

AVERAGES OF DISCRETE DATA

There are three types of averages: <u>mean</u>, <u>median</u> and the <u>mode</u>.

<u>Mean</u> – Sometimes known as the 'average'.

Mean = <u>sum of a set of values</u>
the number of values used

<u>Median</u> – The middle value when the numbers are put in order of size.

<u>Mode</u> – The one that occurs the most often.

<u>Range</u> – This tells us how much the information is spread.

Range = highest value – lowest value

EXAMPLE

A football team scored the following number of goals in their first ten matches:

2, 4, 0, 1, 2, 2, 3, 6, 2, 4

Find the mean, median, mode and range of the number of goals scored.

Mean = $\dfrac{2 + 4 + 0 + 1 + 2 + 2 + 3 + 6 + 2 + 4}{10} = \dfrac{26}{10} = 2.6$ goals

Do not round off

Median =   0, 1, 2, 2, 2, 2, 3, 4, 4, 6   Put in order of size first

6̷ 1̷ 2̷ 2̷ (2 2) 3̷ 4̷ 4̷ 6̷   Cross off from the ends to find the middle

$\dfrac{2 + 2}{2} = 2$ goals

If there are 2 numbers in the middle, the median is halfway between them.

Mode = 2 goals, because it occurs 4 times

Range = 6 – 0 = 6

Remember to subtract the 2 values in order to obtain the range.

EXAMPLE

The mean of four numbers is 20, the mean of six other numbers is 36. What is the mean of all 10 numbers?

The sum of the four numbers is 80 $\left(\dfrac{80}{4} = 20\right)$ The sum of the six numbers is 216 $\left(\dfrac{216}{6} = 36\right)$

Mean of all 10 numbers is 29.6 $\left(\dfrac{\text{total sum}}{10} = \dfrac{80+216}{10} = \dfrac{296}{10} = 29.6\right)$

EXAMPLE

The mean of four numbers is 7. Three of the numbers are 10, 4 and 8. Find the value of the other number.

The sum of the four numbers is 28 $\left(\dfrac{28}{4} = 7\right)$

If x is the missing number $10 + 4 + 8 + x = 28$
$22 + x = 28$
$x = 6$

The other number is 6.

Examiner's Top Tip
When finding the mean of a frequency table, remember to divide by   the sum of the frequencies and not by how many groups there are.

USING APPROPRIATE AVERAGES

- The <u>mean</u> is useful when a typical value is wanted. Be careful not to use the mean if there are extreme values, e.g. for this data 1, 2, 3, 4, 57

- The <u>median</u> is a useful average to use if there are extreme values.

- The <u>mode</u> is useful when the most common value is needed.

AVERAGES ①

FINDING AVERAGES FROM A FREQUENCY TABLE

A frequency table tells us <u>how many</u> are in a group.

Two students were four minutes late.

EXAMPLE

Charlotte made this frequency table for the number of minutes late students were to registration:

Number of minutes late (x)	0	1	2	3	4
Frequency (f)	10	4	6	3	2

MEAN

Mean = $\dfrac{\text{Total of the results when multiplied}}{\text{Total of the frequency}}$

This tells us that four students were one minute late for registration.

$$= \frac{(10 \times 0) + (4 \times 1) + (6 \times 2) + (3 \times 3) + (2 \times 4)}{(10 + 4 + 6 + 3 + 2)}$$

Remember to add up the total frequency.

$$= \frac{0 + 4 + 12 + 9 + 8}{25} = \frac{33}{25} = 1.32 \text{ minutes late}$$

MEDIAN

There are 25 students in the class, the middle person is the 13th.
From the frequency table:

Number of minutes late (x)	0	1	2	3	4
Frequency (f)	10	4	6	3	2

The 13th student is in here.

Median number of minutes late is 1.

The first 10 students

Remember to write down the answer zero, not the number 10 (this is the frequency).

MODE

This is the one that has the highest frequency.
Mode = 0 minutes late because it had a frequency higher than any others.

RANGE = 4 – 0 = 4 minutes.

QUICK TEST

1. Find the mean, median, mode and range of this data:

   2, 4, 1, 1, 2, 3, 7, 5, 5, 5, 2, 5, 6

2. The number of sisters that each student in class 9M has are recorded in the table below:

Number of sisters (x)	0	1	2	3	4	5	6
Frequency (f)	7	9	4	4	2	2	1

   a) Calculate the mean number of sisters that the students have
   b) What is the modal number of sisters?

2. a) 1.83 sisters (2 d.p.) b) 1 sister
1. Mean = 3.7 (1 d.p.), median = 4, mode = 5, range = 6

AVERAGES ②

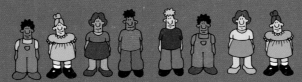

AVERAGES OF GROUPED DATA

MEAN
- When the data is grouped, the exact data is not known.
- Estimate by using the <u>midpoint</u> of the <u>class</u> <u>interval</u>.
- The midpoint is the halfway value.

EXAMPLE
The weight of year 9 pupils.

Weight (kg)	Frequency (f)	Midpoint (χ)	fχ
$40 \leq W < 45$	7	42.5	297.5
$45 \leq W < 50$	4	47.5	190
$50 \leq W < 55$	3	52.5	157.5
$55 \leq W < 60$	1	57.5	57.5

- This is the same as before except the frequency is multiplied by the midpoint.

$$\text{MEAN} = \frac{\sum f\chi}{\sum f} = \frac{(7 \times 42.5) + (4 \times 47.5) + (3 \times 52.5) + (1 \times 57.5)}{7 + 4 + 3 + 1}$$

$$= \frac{702.5}{15} = 46.8 \text{ kg (1 d.p.)}$$

$\sum$ **just means 'sum of'**

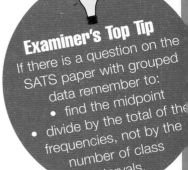

Examiner's Top Tip
If there is a question on the SATS paper with grouped data remember to:
- find the midpoint
- divide by the total of the frequencies, not by the number of class intervals.

MODE
When using grouped data only the <u>modal</u> <u>class</u> can be found. This is the class with the highest frequency.
Modal class = $40 \leq W < 45$

MEDIAN
For grouped data only the class interval containing the median can be found.
There are 15 pupils in the survey above, the middle person is the 8th one.
The 8th person is in the second interval:

$$40 \leq W < 50$$

COMPARING SETS OF DATA

The range and averages are used to compare sets of data.

EXAMPLE

9A obtained a mean of 57% in a test.
9T obtained a mean of 84% in the same test.

Use the range when comparing data.

From the averages we would say 9T is better than 9A.
However if the range is looked at for each class:

9A = 100% – 21% = 79%
9T = 94% – 76% = 18%

Using the range it can be seen that not all of 9T are better than 9A, because some of 9A obtained higher marks than 9T. The average for 9A has been lowered because of the low marks obtained by some pupils.

FINDING THE MEAN FROM A FREQUENCY DIAGRAM

It has been known that you could be asked to estimate the mean from a frequency diagram.

EXAMPLE

This frequency diagram shows some students height. Estimate the mean height.

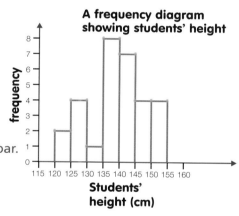

A frequency diagram showing students' height

* Firstly we need to work out the mid-points and frequency of each bar.
* $(122.5 \times 2) + (127.5 \times 4) + (132.5 \times 1) + (137.5 \times 8) + (142.5 \times 7) +$
$(147.5 \times 4) + (152.5 \times 4)$

$\dfrac{\sum fx}{\sum f} = \dfrac{4185}{30}$

The mean height = 139.5 cm

QUICK TEST

LEVEL 7

C) The length of the roots of some plants are recorded in the table below.

Length (cm)	Frequency (f)	Midpoint (χ)
$0 \leq L < 5$	7	
$5 \leq L < 10$	9	
$10 \leq L < 15$	4	
$15 \leq L < 20$	2	

a) Find an estimate for the mean length.

b) What is the modal class?

WHAT IS PROBABILITY?

- This is the chance that something will happen.
- Probabilities must be written as either a <u>fraction</u>, <u>decimal</u> or <u>percentage</u>. Never write the words 'Out of'.
- Probabilities can be shown on a probability scale. All probabilities lie between 0 and 1. No event has a probability greater than 1.

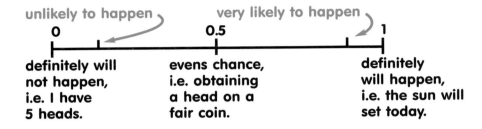

unlikely to happen   very likely to happen

| definitely will not happen, i.e. I have 5 heads. | evens chance, i.e. obtaining a head on a fair coin. | definitely will happen, i.e. the sun will set today. |

EXAMPLE

A bag contains 3 red, 1 blue and 4 yellow beads. If a bead is chosen at random:
a) Mark with an X the probability of choosing a green bead.
b) Mark with a Y the probability of choosing a yellow bead.

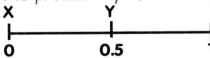

X is at 0 since there are no green beads, i.e. a green will definitely not be chosen.

A yellow bead has an evens chance of being chosen, since half of the beads are yellow.

<u>Exhaustive</u> <u>events</u> account for all possible outcomes, i.e. the list 1, 2, 3, 4, 5, 6 gives all possible outcomes when a fair die is thrown.

PROBABILITY OF AN EVENT NOT HAPPENING

If two events cannot happen at the same time:

<u>P(event will not happen) = 1 – P(event will happen)</u>

To find the probability that an event will not happen:
- Find the probability the event will happen.
- Subtract it from 1.

> Use the fraction key on your calculator to help.

EXAMPLE

The probability that it rains today is $\frac{7}{11}$. What is the probability that it will not rain?

P(not rain) = 1 – P(will rain)

P(not rain) = $1 - \frac{7}{11} = \frac{4}{11}$

EXAMPLE

The probability that the torch works is 0.53. What is the probability that it does not work?

P(does not work) = 1 – P(works)

P(does not work) = 1 – 0.53 = 0.47

> To check quickly, add both numbers up and make sure you get 1.

PROBABILITY IN PRACTICE

- Estimates of probability can be carried out by experiment or surveys.

EXAMPLE

It could be said that the next car to pass the school is blue only after a survey has been conducted.

CALCULATING PROBABILITIES

- Probabilities can be calculated using the fact that each outcome is equally likely.

Probability of an event = $\dfrac{\text{Number of ways an event can happen}}{\text{Total number of outcomes}}$

P(event) is the shortened way of writing the probability of an event.

EXAMPLE

There are 12 socks in a drawer: three are red, four are blue and the rest are black. Nigel picks out a sock at random. What is the probability that the sock he has pulled out is
a) blue   b) red   c) black   d) blue, red or black   e) green

a) $P(\text{blue}) = \frac{4}{12} = \frac{1}{3}$
b) $P(\text{red}) = \frac{3}{12} = \frac{1}{4}$
c) $P(\text{black}) = \frac{5}{12}$
d) $P(\text{blue, red or black}) = \frac{12}{12} = 1$
e) $P(\text{green}) = 0$

There are no green socks in the drawer so the event will definitely not happen.

All probabilities add up to 1, i.e. choosing a blue, red or black sock will definitely happen.

Make sure that the number on the bottom is the total number of outcomes.

Examiner's Top Tip
Whenever you do a question on probability, check that your answer is not greater than 1. If it is you've done it wrong, so go back and try again.

PROBABILITY ①

QUICK TEST

1. On the number line below, place the arrows on the scale to show these probabilities:

   a) I will obtain a head or tail if I throw a fair coin

   b) I will grow wings by 6 p.m. today

   c) I will get an even number if I throw a fair die.

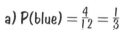

2. A bag has three red, four green and 10 yellow beads in it. If Reece takes out a bead at random, what is the probability that it is:

   a) a red bead   b) a green bead   c) a red or green bead

   d) a pink bead   e) a red, green or yellow bead?

3. The probability that somebody leaves a message on an answering machine is 0.32.

   What is the probability that they do not leave a message?

3. 0.68
2. a) $\frac{3}{17}$ b) $\frac{4}{17}$ c) $\frac{7}{17}$ d) 0 e) $\frac{17}{17} = 1$
1. b)
c)
a)

PROBABILITY ②

POSSIBLE OUTCOMES FOR TWO EVENTS

• *Using lists, diagrams and tables is helpful when there are outcomes of two events.*

EXAMPLE (LISTS)

For his lunch Matthew can choose a main course and a pudding.
List all the possible outcomes of his lunch.

Menu	
Main Courses	**Puddings**
Pizza	Apple pie
Chicken	Lemon tart
Salad	

Pizza, Apple pie   Chicken, Apple pie   Salad, Apple pie

Pizza, Lemon tart   Chicken, Lemon tart   Salad, Lemon tart

There are 6 possible outcomes.

Try and write out the outcomes in a well-ordered way.

EXAMPLE (SAMPLE SPACE DIAGRAM)

The spinner and the die are thrown together, and their scores are added.
Represent the outcomes on a <u>sample space diagram</u>.

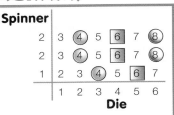

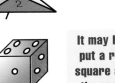

• There are 18 outcomes.
a) The P(score of 6) = $\frac{3}{18}$ = $\frac{1}{6}$
b) The P(multiple of 4) = $\frac{5}{18}$

2 on the spinner, 6 on the die, 2 + 6 = 8

It may help to put a ring or square around the numbers you need.

EXAMPLE (TWO WAY TABLE)

The diagram shows a two way table for pupils in a class who are studying either French or German.

Language	Male	Female	Total
French	7	17	24
German	4	6	10
Total	11	23	34

a) *If a person is chosen at random, what is the probability that they do French?*
   P(French) = $\frac{24}{34}$ = $\frac{12}{17}$
b) *If a girl is chosen at random, what is the probability that she does German?*
   P(German) = $\frac{6}{23}$ ← 6 girls do German
   23 girls in total

EXAMPLE (TREE DIAGRAM)

For a tree diagram, probabilities are written on the branches, and <u>multiplied</u> *to obtain the final total.*
The probability that Carlos is late for registration is 0.3.
Find the probability that on two successive days Carlos is late.
Probability that Carlos is late on only one of the days is: 0.21 + 0.21 = 0.42
Probability that Carlos is late on both days is 0.09

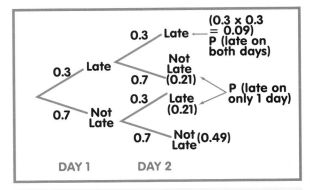

Warning!
• You <u>multiply</u> along the branches.
• You <u>add</u> in order to combine alternative end points.

EXPECTED NUMBER

- Probability can be used to estimate the expected number of times an event is likely to occur.

EXAMPLE
If a die is thrown 180 times, approximately how many two's am I likely to obtain?

Remember there are six outcomes on a die. → $P(2) = \frac{1}{6} \times 180 = 30$ two's

Key in on the calculator: $1 \div 6 \times 180 =$
or do: $180 \div 6 =$

Since a 2 is expected $\frac{1}{6}$ of the time.

EXAMPLE
The probability that Ellie obtains full marks in a spelling test is 0.4. If she takes 30 spelling tests in a year, in how many tests would you expect her to make no mistakes?
$0.4 \times 30 = 12$ tests

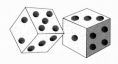

Examiner's Top Tip
Be careful when there are two events. Use one of the different ways to show the information – this should make calculating probabilities easier.

RELATIVE FREQUENCIES

- If a die is thrown 180 times, we have shown that approximately 30 two's would be obtained. When experiments like this are used to estimate probabilities it is known as the <u>relative frequency</u> that the event will happen.

Relative frequency of an event =

$$\frac{\text{Number of times the event occurred}}{\text{Total number of trials}}$$

Relative frequency is used as an estimate of probability.

- As the number of throws increases, the relative frequency will get closer to the expected probability.

EXAMPLE
When a fair coin was thrown 80 times, a head came up 35 times. What is the relative frequency of getting a head?
Number of trials = 80   Relative frequency = $\frac{35}{80}$ = 0.4375
Number of heads = 35

The <u>theoretical</u> probability = $\frac{1}{2}$ = 0.5

QUICK TEST

1. The probability that you pass a driving test on the first attempt is 0.35. If 200 people are taking their driving test, how many would you expect to pass first time?
2. A fair die is thrown 600 times. If a 5 comes up 88 times what is the relative frequency?
3. Two fair die are thrown together and their totals multiplied. Complete the sample space diagram. a) What is the probability of a total of 12? b) What is the probability that the total is a multiple of 4?

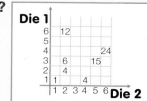

Die 1

	1	2	3	4	5	6
6	12					
5						
4					24	
3	6		15			
2	4					
1	1		4			

Die 2

1. 70 2. $\frac{11}{75}$ 3. a) $\frac{1}{36}$ b) $\frac{15}{36} = \frac{5}{12}$

HANDLING DATA

1. The frequency table shows the hair colour of 20 pupils

Hair colour	Brown	Black	Auburn	Blonde
Frequency	9	6	3	2

a) Draw a pictogram of this information. Let 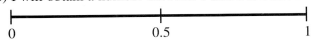 represent 2 pupils.
b) Draw a bar chart of this information.

2. On the number line below, place the arrows on the scale to show these probabilities:
a) I will obtain an even number if I throw a fair die.
b) I will have two heads by 5 p.m. today.
c) I will obtain a number between 1 and 6 if I throw a fair die.

```
├─────────────────┼─────────────────┤
0               0.5                 1
```

3. Write down an event which has a probability of 0.

....

4. Write down an event which has a probability of 1.

....

C 5. A chocolate firm asked 720 students which type of chocolate they preferred. The pie chart shows the results. How many people preferred:
a) White chocolate ....
b) Fruit and nut ....
c) Milk chocolate ....

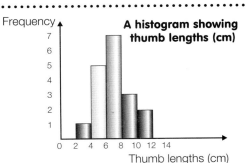

6. The letters M A T H E M A T I C S are placed on separate pieces of card and put into a bag. Reece picks out a card at random.
What is the probability that he picks:
a) a letter T ....
b) a letter M ....
c) the letters A or C ....

7. Find the mean, median, mode and range of this data:
2, 4, 1, 1, 2, 3, 7, 5, 5, 5, 2, 5, 6

C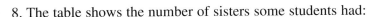

8. The table shows the number of sisters some students had:

C

Sisters (x)	0	1	2	3	4
Frequency (y)	5	15	9	2	1

Calculate the mean number of sisters.

9. The probability that I receive a letter is 32%. What is the probability that I do not receive a letter?

....

10. a) Using the histogram, complete the frequency table:

Thumb length (cm)	Frequency
$2 \leq L < 4$	
$4 \leq L < 6$	
$6 \leq L < 8$	7
$8 \leq L < 10$	
$10 \leq L < 12$	

A histogram showing thumb lengths (cm)

b) How many people were in the survey?
c) Draw a frequency polygon on the histogram.

C = A calculator may be used   **7** = This question is for Level 7 students

11. a) Describe the correlation of the scatter diagram.
b) Draw on the line of best fit.

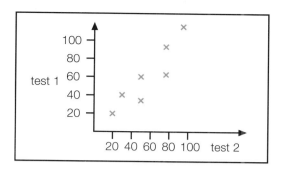

test 1
100
80
60
40
20

20 40 60 80 100   test 2

12. The probability of passing a driving test is 0.7.
If 200 people take the test today, how many would you expect to pass?

....

13. The diagram shows a two-way table for pupils in a class, who are studying either Italian or Spanish.

	Male	Female	Total
Italian	5	10	15
Spanish	12	4	16
Total	17	14	31

a) If a person is chosen at random, what is the probability that they do Spanish? ....
b) If a girl is chosen at random, what is the probability that she does Italian? ....

14. The length of roots of some plants is recorded in the table below:

Length (cm)	Frequency	Midpoint (x)
$0 \leq l < 5$	6	
$5 \leq l < 10$	9	
$10 \leq l < 15$	15	
$15 \leq l < 20$	9	
$20 \leq l < 25$	6	
$25 \leq l < 30$	2	

a) Find an estimate for the mean length ....
b) What is the modal class? ....

15. A fair spinner is labelled as shown. The results of the first 12 spins are:
A B B C A D C C A D B A

A	B
D	C

a) Write down the relative frequency of the letter A for these results ....
b) As the number of results increases, what do you expect to happen to the relative frequency of the letter A?

....

16. This question was included in a survey. 'Do you agree that swimming lessons should only take place on a Saturday morning?' What is wrong with the question?

....

17. The probability that a bus is late is 0.4. By drawing a tree diagram or otherwise, calculate the probability that the bus is late on two consecutive days.

....

How did you do?

1–4	correct	....start again
5–8	correct	....getting there
8–13	correct	....good work
14–17	correct	....excellent

MIXED QUESTIONS

1. Work out the answers to these questions. Show your working:
a) 53 x 7 ....
b) 162 ÷ 9 ....
c) 813 – 354 ....

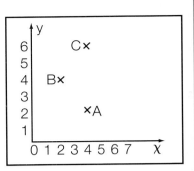

2. Write down the coordinates of A, B and C
Plot the point D so that the shape formed when the points are joined up is a square.
What are the coordinates of D? ....

3. The temperature in Manchester last night was –3°C. If the temperature rises by 12°C what is the temperature now?

....

4. A box of chocolates contains 15 hard centres and 13 soft centres.
One chocolate is chosen at random; work out the probability that it will be:
a) a hard centre ....
b) a soft centre ....
c) a mint ....

5. On the square, draw on all the lines of symmetry.
What is the order of rotational symmetry? ....

6. Imran has a bag of sweets (s). Write an expression for each of the following:
a) Jonathan has four more sweets than Imran ....
b) Susan has twice as many sweets as Imran ....
c) Matthew has half as many sweets as Jonathan ....

7. Solve the following equations:
a) $2X + 10 = 22$ ....
b) $5X – 1 = 3x + 11$ ....

8. Work out:

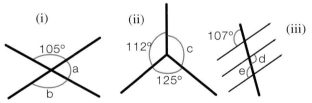

(i) 105° a b
(ii) 112° c 125°
(iii) 107° d e

9. Work out the answers to
a) 493 x 78 ....
b) 45$\overline{)1215}$ ....

10. The probability that Emily misses the bus is $\frac{7}{15}$. What is the probability that she does not miss the bus?

....

11. Kelly says that when she spins the spinner, the probability that she gets a 4 is $\frac{1}{3}$. Why is she wrong?

....

12. Charlotte carried out a survey to find out the favourite flavours of crisps in her class. The results are shown in the table below:

Crisp flavour	Frequency
Cheese	7
Salt 'n' vinegar	10
Beef	6
Smoky Bacon	1

Draw a pie chart of this information.

(c) = A calculator may be used (7) = This question is for Level 7 students

13. The 'Good Shoe Shop' is having a sale: '30% off everything'. Calculate the sale price of a pair of shoes costing £40.

....

14. Write down the nth term of this sequence.
7, 10, 13, 16, ...

15. Work out the volume of this 3D solid, giving your answer to 1 d.p.

.... 12.1cm

16. Mr Riches shares £125 000 between his two sisters in the ratio 11 : 14. Work out how much each receives.

....

10.9 cm

8.7 cm

17. Sketch the graphs of
a) y = 3x − 4
b) y = 4 − 2x
Write down the gradient and intercept of each one

18. If a = 4, b = 3.2 and c = 6.5, evaluate the expression: $\dfrac{a^2\,b}{2a - 3b + 4c^2}$

....

19. Solve the simultaneous equations:
3x + y = 20 ....
5x − 2y = 26 ....

20. A ladder rests against a wall so that the foot of the ladder is 6.5 m from the wall. If the ladder is 18 m long, calculate the height up the wall the ladder reaches.

21. The lengths of some seedlings are measured.

Length (cm)	Frequency
$0 \leq L < 10$	5
$10 \leq L < 20$	22
$20 \leq L < 30$	13
$30 \leq L < 40$	5

Calculate an estimate for the mean length of the seedlings.

....

22. Frances weighs 55 kg, correct to the nearest kilogram. What are the upper and lower limits of her weight?

....

23. The equation $x^3 − 5x = 10$ has a solution between 2 and 3. By using a trial and improvement method, find the solution to one decimal place.

....

....

How did you do?

1–6	correct	....start again
7–12	correct	....getting there
13–17	correct	....good work
18–23	correct	....excellent

Number

1. Three million, two hundred and forty-eight thousand and twenty.

2. a) 6512   b) 4181   c) 22813   d) 215

3. 7°C

4. a) 60 b) 60 c) 130 d) 100 e) 300 f) 1400 g) 7000 h) 9000

5. a) 3, 6, 9, 12 b) 2, 3, 5, 7, 11 c) 1, 2, 4, 5, 10

6. 2 x 2 x 2 x 3 = 2^3 x 3

7. a) 10 b) 36 c) 6 d) 8

8. 2.76 x 10^9

9. a) x = 24   b) y = 25   c) z = 152

10. 12%

11. 1404p or £14.04

12. 18 tins

13. a) 15 b) 4 c) –10 d) –20

14. £38.25

15. 600

16. 24%

17. 36 cm

18. a) $\frac{1}{3}$ b) $\frac{7}{20}$ c) $\frac{6}{13}$ d) $\frac{16}{27}$

19. a) 12.69 b) 28.76 c) 2.94

20. a) 273 000 b) 0.000786 c) 27 100

21.

Fraction	Decimal	Percentage
$\frac{3}{4}$	0.75	75%
$\frac{2}{5}$	0.4	40%
$\frac{1}{3}$	$0.\dot{3}$	$33.\dot{3}$%

22. £6498.89

23. 0.274, $\frac{4}{7}$, 61%, $\frac{9}{10}$, 0.93, 94%

24. a) 0.006 b) 4 c) 50000

25. a) 14.45 (2 d.p.)   b) 769.6 (1 d.p.)

26. $\dfrac{30^2 + 100}{2 \times 5} = \dfrac{1000}{10} = 100$

Algebra

1. a) r + 5 b) y – 7 c) $\frac{p}{4}$ d) $\frac{r-4}{s}$

2. a) 10a b) 6a + 3b c) $5xy$ d) 10ab e) $12a^2$ f) 6a + b

3. 8a + 10b + 5

4. a)

n	1	2	3	4	5	6
p	6	10	14	18	22	26

b) p = 4n + 2

5. a) 4 b) 0 c) 17 d) 6

6. a) 320 b) 900

7. a) 4n + 8 b) n^2 c) 2n – 2 d) 4n + 2

8. a) n = 16 b) n = 6 c) a = 1 d) n = 35

9. a), b) and d)

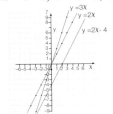

c) y = 3x is steeper than y = 2x, since it has a bigger gradient

10. a) n = 3 b) n = –5 c) n = –14

11. a) 4n + 10 b) 4n + 10 = 22   n = 3

12. 2n + 3

13. a) 5 (x + 3) b) 6 (x – 2) c) 4 ($3x$ + 5)

14. a) Gradient = 4; intercept = (0, 10)
b) Gradient = –2; intercept = (0, 6)

15. a) $66.\dot{6}$ m.p.h. b) 1 hour c) 50 m.p.h. d) 1442

16. x = –3, y = 4

17. a) n < $\frac{4}{3}$ b) n ≤ 2

18. n^2 + 2

19. x = 3 (y + 6)

Shape, Space and Measures

1. a) mm b) kg c) m d) ml e) m

2. A = 9.2 B = 9.5 C = 2.42 D = 2.46 E = 2.48 F = 6.25
G = 6.75

3. a)
b) 2

4. a) order 1 or no rotational symmetry
b) order 4   c) order 4

5. acute: 41°, 72°, 83°   obtuse: 127°   reflex: 241°, 379°
right-angled: 90°

6. i) a = 80° ii) b = 155° iii) c = 138° d = 42°
iv) e = 65° v) f = 102° vi) g = 60° h = 60° i = 120°

7. 14 cm³

8. a) 6.2 kg   b) 42 mm   c) 10.5 pints (approx)

9.

   plan   elevation from A   elevation from B

10. a) 27 cm²   b) 44 cm²   c) 36 cm³

11. a) 68.0 cm²   b) 63.6 cm²   c) 63.6 cm²   d) 208 cm²

12. 30.8 cm (1 d.p.)

13. 17.584 cm²

14. a) 110°   b) 240°   c) 140°

15.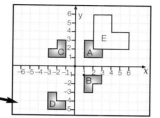

16. a) 601 cm³ (3 s.f.)   b) 1750 cm³ (3 s.f.)

17. a) 16.6 m   b) 10.7 m

18. 81.98 m² (2 d.p.)

19. 70 000 cm²

20. 56 m²

21. $9.15 \leq 9.2 < 9.25$

22. A = (3, 0, 0)   B = (3, 1, 0)
     C = (3, 1, 2)   D = (0, 0, 3)
     E = (1, 1, 3)   F = (1, 0, 2)

Handling Data

1. a)  b)

2.

5. a) 240   b) 180   c) 300

6. a) $\frac{2}{11}$ b) $\frac{2}{11}$ c) $\frac{3}{11}$

7. mean = 3.7 (1 d.p.)   median = 4   mode = 5   range = 6

8. mean = 1.34 sisters (2 d.p.)

9. 68% = 0.68

10. a)
Thumb length (cm)	Frequency
$2 \leq L < 4$	1
$4 \leq L < 6$	5
$6 \leq L < 8$	7
$8 \leq L < 10$	3
$10 \leq L < 12$	2

  b) 18

c)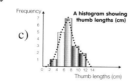

11. a) Positive correlation:
the better you did in test
1 the better you did in test 2
b)

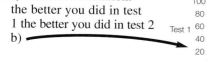

12. 140 people

13. a) $\frac{16}{31}$ b) $\frac{10}{14} = \frac{5}{7}$

14. a) mean = 13.1 cm (3 s.f.)   b) modal class = $10 \leq L < 15$

15. a) $\frac{4}{12} = \frac{1}{3}$ b) approach the expected probability of $\frac{1}{4}$

16. Your opinion that you only want swimming lessons on a Saturday morning is evident.

17. $0.4 \times 0.4 = 0.16$

Mixed

1. a) 371   b) 18   c) 459

2. A = (4, 2)   B = (2, 4)   C = (4, 6)   D should be at (6, 4)

3. 9°C

4. a) hard = $\frac{15}{28}$ b) soft = $\frac{13}{28}$ c) mint = 0

5. Rotational symmetry order 4

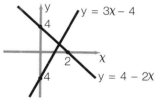

6. a) $s + 4$ b) $2s$ c) $\frac{s + 4}{2}$

7. a) x = 6   b) x = 6

8. i) a = 75° b = 105°   ii) c = 123°   iii) d = 73° e = 107°

9. a) 38 454   b) 27

10. $\frac{8}{15}$

11. Because a 4 takes up half of the available space. Hence P(4) = $\frac{1}{2}$

12. Pie chart should be drawn with the following angles: Cheese = 105° Salt 'n' vinegar = 150° Beef = 90° Smoky Bacon = 15°

13. £28

14. 3n + 4

15. 573.7 cm³ (1 d.p.)

16. £55 000, £70 000

17. y = 3x – 4, Gradient = 3   y = 4 – 2x, Gradient = –2
    Intercept = (0, –4)   Intercept = (0, 4)

18. 0.306 (3 s.f.)

19. x = 6   y = 2

20. 16.8 metres (1 d.p.)

21. mean = 19 cm

22. $54.5 \leq$ weight < 55.5

23. x = 2.9 (1 d.p.)